Hoem

D0479383

How to Use SPSS®

A Step-by-Step Guide to Analysis and Interpretation

Fifth Edition

Brian C. Cronk
Missouri Western State University

Pyrczak Publishing
P.O. Box 250430 ❖ Glendale, CA 91225

Notice

SPSS is a registered trademark of SPSS, Inc. Screen images © by SPSS, Inc. and Microsoft Corporation. Used with permission.

This book is not approved or sponsored by SPSS.

"Pyrczak Publishing" is an imprint of Fred Pyrczak, Publisher, A California Corporation.

Although the author and publisher have made every effort to ensure the accuracy and completeness of information contained in this book, we assume no responsibility for errors, inaccuracies, omissions, or any inconsistency herein. Any slights of people, places, or organizations are unintentional.

Project Director: Monica Lopez.

Consulting Editors: George Burruss, Jose L. Galvan, Matthew Giblin, Deborah M. Oh, Jack Petit, and Richard Rasor.

Editorial assistance provided by Cheryl Alcorn, Randall R. Bruce, Karen M. Disner, Brenda Koplin, Erica Simmons, and Sharon Young.

Cover design by Robert Kibler and Larry Nichols.

Printed in the United States of America by Malloy, Inc.

Copyright © 2008, 2006, 2004, 2002, 1999 by Fred Pyrczak, Publisher. All rights reserved. No portion of this book may be reproduced or transmitted in any form or by any means without the prior written permission of the publisher.

ISBN 1-884585-79-5

Table of Contents

Introduction to the Fifth Edition

The SPSS statistical package is designed to perform a wide range of statistical procedures. As with any other powerful computer software, there are certain conventions and techniques that must be mastered for efficient use of the software and to obtain consistently correct answers. By providing detailed, step-by-step guidance illustrated with examples, this book will help you attain such mastery.

In addition to showing you how to enter data and obtain results, this book explains how to select appropriate statistics and present the results in a form that is suitable for use in a research report in the social or behavioral sciences. For instance, the section on the independent t test shows how to state (i.e., phrase) the results of both a significant and an insignificant test.

What's New?

The Fifth Edition represents another major change in this text. All of the screenshots have been upgraded for Version 15.0 of the software. The screenshots are now tailored for the student version of the software (except for Sections 6.7, 6.8, and 6.10, which require modules not included in the student version). Version 15.0 introduced major changes in the way that SPSS makes graphs, and these changes are now included in a completely revised Chapter 4. Finally, the number of screenshots has been increased to make certain sections of the text clearer.

Audience

This book is ideal as a supplement to traditional introductory and intermediate-level statistics textbooks. It can also be used as a statistics refresher manual in a research methods course. Finally, students can use it as a desk reference guide in a variety of workplace settings after they graduate from college.

SPSS is an incredibly powerful program, and this text does not attempt to be a comprehensive user's manual. Instead, the emphasis is on the procedures normally covered in introductory and intermediate-level courses in statistics and research methods.

Organization

This book is divided into eight chapters. The first two chapters deal with the basic mechanics of using the SPSS program. Each of the remaining chapters focuses on a particular class of statistics.

Each chapter contains several short sections. For the most part, these sections are self-contained. However, students are expected to master the SPSS basics in Chapters 1 and 2 before attempting to learn the skills presented in the rest of the book. Except for the skills in the first two chapters, this book can be used in a nonlinear manner. Thus, an instructor can assign the first two chapters early in a course, then assign other sections in whatever order is appropriate to the course.

Appendix A contains a discussion of effect size. Appendix B contains data sets that are needed for the Practice Exercises interspersed throughout this book. The glossary in Appendix C provides definitions of most of the statistical terms used in this book. Because it is assumed that this text is being used in conjunction with a main statistics textbook, the glossary definitions are brief and are designed to serve only as reminders. Appendix D provides the sample data files that are used throughout this book. Appendices E and F provide information for users of earlier versions of SPSS.

SPSS Versions

There are numerous versions of the SPSS statistical package. This book was written for use with SPSS for Windows Student Version 15.0. If you are using an earlier version of SPSS, Appendix E describes some of the differences.

SPSS also offers several modules. Most institutions have at least the Base, Regression, and Advanced modules installed. With these three modules, you can conduct all of the analyses in this text. If you are using the student version of SPSS, some procedures will not be available. When this is the case, the text will clearly indicate that another product is necessary.

If you have different add-on modules installed, the menu bars shown in the illustrations of this text may appear slightly different. If your menu bars look different or if you cannot locate a menu item for a command presented in this book, it may be that your institution supports different modules. Ask your instructor for additional guidance.

Availability of SPSS

Some institutions purchase site licenses from SPSS to provide the software at no charge to their faculty and, sometimes, to their students. If your institution has not purchased a site license, you should still be able to purchase the student version of the software in your campus bookstore at a price discounted for the educational community. Either of these will be a fully functional version of the software intended for your personal use. However, the student version is limited to 50 variables and 1,500 cases.

Conventions

The following conventions have been used throughout this book:

- Items in **bold** are defined in the glossary in Appendix C.
- Items in *italics* are either buttons or menus from the SPSS program, or they are statistical symbols.
- Items in ALL CAPITAL LETTERS are either acronyms or the names of variables in the SPSS data file.

Screenshots

Screenshots have been used extensively throughout the text to visually represent what is described. In some instances, there may be minor differences between screenshots shown in the text and on the student's own screen. Because no two Windows computers are configured exactly alike, and because different revision levels of the SPSS program itself can produce slightly modified screen images, such minor differences are unavoidable.

Practice Exercises

Practice Exercises are included for each skill presented. In addition, the skills acquired in this text can be used in practice exercises in other statistics texts or workbooks. One text that would work well in this capacity is *Real Data: A Statistics Workbook Based on Empirical Data.*[1]

Acknowledgments

This book is dedicated to the students in my Introductory Psychological Statistics and Research Methods Laboratory courses. While teaching those courses, I became aware of the need for an SPSS manual that did more than simply tell students how to start the program and enter data. I am deeply indebted to Wendy Schweigert at Bradley University, who first showed me the power, simplicity, and usefulness of statistics. I would also like to thank the hundreds of instructors who adopted previous editions of this text and provided me with constructive feedback to make this edition better. Of course, this text would not have been possible without the support of my entire family. Every day, I am thankful for Bobbie, Jonathan, and Katherine.

Brian C. Cronk

---

[1] Holcomb, Z. (1997). *Real Data: A Statistics Workbook Based on Empirical Data.* Los Angeles: Pyrczak Publishing.

Notes

Chapter 1

Getting Started

Section 1.1   Starting SPSS

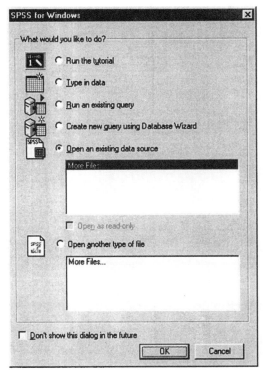

Startup procedures for SPSS will differ slightly, depending on the exact configuration of the machine on which it is installed. On most computers, you can start SPSS by clicking on *Start*, then clicking on *Programs*, then on *SPSS*. On many installations, there will be an *SPSS* icon on the desktop that you can double-click to start the program.

When SPSS is started, you may be presented with the dialog box to the left, depending on the options your system administrator selected for your version of the program. If you have the dialog box, click *Type in data* and *OK*, which will present a blank **data window**.[1]

If you were not presented with the **dialog box** to the left, SPSS should open automatically with a blank **data window**.

The **data window** and the **output window** provide the basic interface for SPSS. A blank **data window** is shown below.

Section 1.2   Entering Data

One of the keys to success with SPSS is knowing how it stores and uses your data. To illustrate the basics of data entry with SPSS, we will use Example 1.2.1.

Example 1.2.1

A survey was given to several students from four different classes (Tues/Thurs mornings, Tues/Thurs afternoons, Mon/Wed/Fri mornings, and Mon/Wed/Fri afternoons). The students were asked

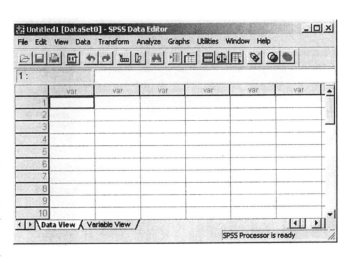

---

[1] Items that appear in the glossary are presented in **bold**. *Italics* are used to indicate menu items.

whether or not they were "morning people" and whether or not they worked. This survey also asked for their final grade in the class (100% being the highest grade possible). The response sheets from two students are presented below:

Response Sheet 1
ID:	4593		
Day of class:	_____ MWF	_X_ TTh	
Class time:	_____ Morning	_X_ Afternoon	
Are you a morning person?	_____ Yes	_X_ No	
Final grade in class:	85%		
Do you work outside school?	_____ Full-time	_____ Part-time	
	_X_ No		

Response Sheet 2
ID:	1901		
Day of class:	_X_ MWF	___ TTh	
Class time:	_X_ Morning	___ Afternoon	
Are you a morning person?	_X_ Yes	___ No	
Final grade in class:	83%		
Do you work outside school?	_____ Full-time	_X_ Part-time	
	_____ No		

Our goal is to enter the data from the two students into SPSS for use in future analyses. The first step is to determine the variables that need to be entered. Any information that can vary among participants is a variable that needs to be considered. Example 1.2.2 lists the variables we will use.

Example 1.2.2

ID
Day of class
Class time
Morning person
Final grade
Whether or not the student works outside school

In the SPSS **data window**, columns represent variables and rows represent participants. Therefore, we will be creating a data file with six columns (variables) and two rows (students/participants).

Section 1.3   Defining Variables

Before we can enter any data, we must first enter some basic information about each variable into SPSS. For instance, variables must first be given names that:

- begin with a letter;
- do not contain a space.

Thus, the variable name "Q7" is acceptable, while the variable name "7Q" is not. Similarly, the variable name "PRE_TEST" is acceptable, but the variable name "PRE TEST" is not. Capitalization does not matter, but variable names are capitalized in this text to make it clear when we are referring to a variable name, even if the variable name is not necessarily capitalized in screenshots.

To define a variable, click on the *Variable View* tab at the bottom of the main screen. This will show you the *Variable View* window. (To return to the *Data View* window, click on the *Data View* tab.)

From the *Variable View* screen, SPSS allows you to create and edit all of the variables in your data file. Each column represents some property of a variable, and each row represents a variable. All variables must be given a name. To do that, click on the first empty cell in the *Name* column and type a valid SPSS variable name. The program will then fill in default values for most of the other properties.

One useful function of SPSS is the ability to define variable and value labels. Variable labels allow you to associate a description with each variable. These descriptions can describe the variables themselves or the values of the variables.

Value labels allow you to associate a description with each value of a variable. For example, for most procedures, SPSS requires numerical values. Thus, for data such as the day of the class (i.e., Mon/Wed/Fri and Tues/Thurs), we need to first code the values as numbers. We can assign the number 1 to Mon/Wed/Fri and the number 2 to Tues/Thurs. To help us keep track of the numbers we have assigned to the values, we use value labels.

To assign value labels, click in the cell you want to assign values to in the *Values* column. This will bring up a small gray button (see arrow, below at left). Click on that button to bring up the Value Labels **dialog box**.

When you enter a value label, you must click *Add* after each entry. This will move the value and its associated label into the bottom section of the window. When all labels have been added, click *OK* to return to the *Variable View* window.

Do not do

In addition to naming and labeling the variable, you have the option of defining the variable type. To do so, simply click on the *Type*, *Width*, or *Decimals* columns in the *Variable View* window. The default value is a numeric field that is eight digits wide with two decimal places displayed. If your data are more than eight digits to the left of the decimal place, they will be displayed in scientific notation (e.g., the number 2,000,000,000 will be displayed as 2.00E+09).[2] SPSS maintains accuracy beyond two decimal places, but all output will be rounded to two decimal places unless otherwise indicated in the *Decimals* column.

In our example, we will be using numeric variables with all of the default values.

Practice Exercise

Create a data file for the six variables and two sample students presented in Example 1.2.1. Name your variables: ID, DAY, TIME, MORNING, GRADE, and WORK. You should code DAY as 1 = Mon/Wed/Fri, 2 = Tues/Thurs. Code TIME as 1 = morning, 2 = afternoon. Code MORNING as 0 = No, 1 = Yes. Code WORK as 0 = No, 1 = Part-Time, 2 = Full-Time. Be sure you enter value labels for the different variables. Note that because value labels are not appropriate for ID and GRADE, these are not coded. When done, your *Variable View* window should look like the screenshot below:

1st

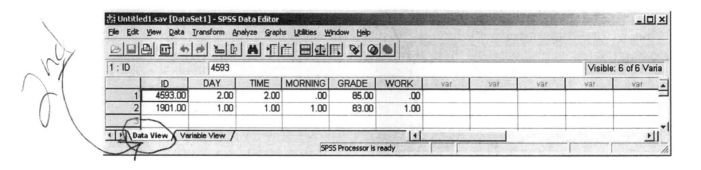

Click on the *Data View* tab to open the data-entry screen. Enter data horizontally, beginning with the first student's ID number. Enter the code for each variable in the appropriate column; to enter the GRADE variable value, enter the student's class grade.

2nd

---

[2] Depending upon your version of SPSS, it may be displayed as 2.0E + 009.

The previous **data window** can be changed to look instead like the screenshot below by clicking on the *Value Labels* icon (see arrow). In this case, the cells display value labels rather than the corresponding codes. If data is entered in this mode, it is not necessary to enter codes, as clicking the button which appears in each cell as the cell is selected will present a drop-down list of the predefined labels. You may use either method, according to your preference.

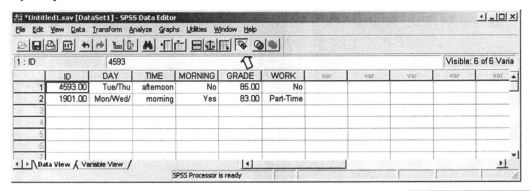

Instead of clicking the *Value Labels* icon, you may optionally toggle between views by clicking *Value Labels* under the *View* menu.

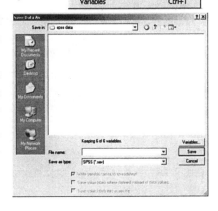

Section 1.4 Loading and Saving Data Files

Once you have entered your data, you will need to save it with a unique name for later use so that you can retrieve it when necessary.

Loading and saving SPSS data files works in the same way as most Windows-based software. Under the *File* menu, there are *Open*, *Save*, and *Save As* commands. SPSS data files have a ".sav" extension, which is added by default to the end of the filename. This tells Windows that the file is an SPSS data file.

Save Your Data

When you save your data file (by clicking *File*, then clicking *Save* or *Save As* to specify a unique name), pay special attention to where you save it. Most systems default to the location <c:\program files\spss>. You will probably want to save your data on a floppy disk, CD-R, or removable USB drive so that you can take the file with you.

Load Your Data

When you load your data (by clicking *File*, then clicking *Open*, then *Data*, or by clicking the open file folder icon), you get a similar window. This window lists all files with the ".sav" extension. If you have trouble locating your saved file, make sure you are looking in the right directory.

Practice Exercise

To be sure that you have mastered saving and opening data files, name your sample data file "SAMPLE" and save it to a removable storage medium. Once it is saved, SPSS will display the name of the file at the top of the **data window**. It is wise to save your work frequently, in case of computer crashes. Note that filenames may be upper- or lowercase. In this text, uppercase is used for clarity.

After you have saved your data, exit SPSS (by clicking *File*, then *Exit*). Restart SPSS and load your data by selecting the "SAMPLE.sav" file you just created.

Section 1.5   Running Your First Analysis

Any time you open a **data window**, you can run any of the analyses available. To get started, we will calculate the students' average grade. (With only two students, you can easily check your answer by hand, but imagine a data file with 10,000 student records.)

The majority of the available statistical tests are under the *Analyze* menu. This menu displays all the options available for your version of the SPSS program (the menus in this book were created with SPSS Student Version 15.0). Other versions may have slightly different sets of options.

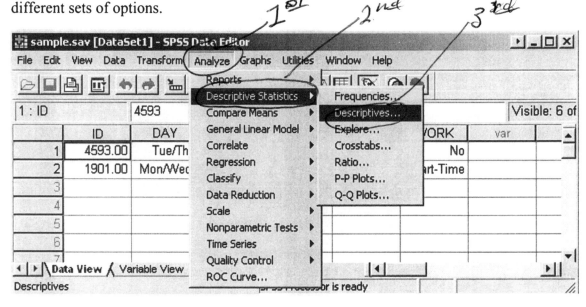

To calculate a **mean** (average), we are asking the computer to summarize our data set. Therefore, we run the command by clicking *Analyze*, then *Descriptive Statistics,* then *Descriptives*.

This brings up the Descriptives **dialog box**. Note that the left side of the box contains a list of all the variables in our data file. On the right is an area labeled *Variable(s)*, where we can specify the variables we would like to use in this particular analysis.

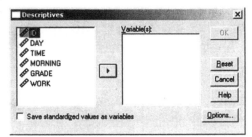

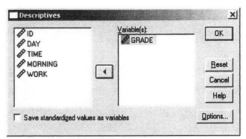

We want to compute the **mean** for the variable called GRADE. Thus, we need to select the variable name in the left window (by clicking on it). To transfer it to the right window, click on the right arrow between the two windows. The arrow always points to the window opposite the highlighted item and can be used to transfer selected variables in either direction. Note that double-clicking on the variable name will also transfer the variable to the opposite window. Standard Windows conventions of "Shift" clicking or "Ctrl" clicking to select multiple variables can be used as well.

When we click on the *OK* button, the analysis will be conducted, and we will be ready to examine our output.

Section 1.6   Examining and Printing Output Files

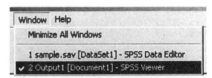

After an analysis is performed, the output is placed in the **output window**, and the **output window** becomes the active window. If this is the first analysis you have conducted since starting SPSS, then a new **output window** will be created. If you have run previous analyses and saved them, your output is added to the end of your previous output.

To switch back and forth between the **data window** and the **output window**, select the desired window from the *Window* menu bar (see arrow, below).

The **output window** is split into two sections. The left section is an outline of the output (SPSS refers to this as the "outline view"). The right section is the output itself.

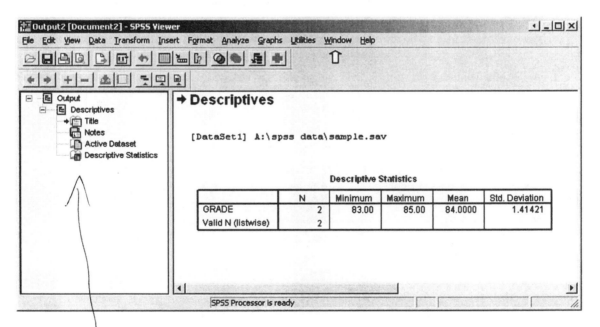

The section on the left of the **output window** provides an outline of the entire **output window**. All of the analyses are listed in the order in which they were conducted. Note that this outline can be used to quickly locate a section of the output. Simply click on the section you would like to see, and the right window will jump to the appropriate place.

Clicking on a statistical procedure also selects all of the output for that command. By pressing the *Delete* key, that output can be deleted from the **output window**. This is a quick way to be sure that the **output window** contains only the desired output. Output can also be selected and pasted into a word processor by clicking *Edit*, then *Copy Objects* to copy the output. You can then switch to your word processor and click *Edit,* then *Paste.*

To print your output, simply click *File*, then *Print*, or click on the printer icon on the toolbar. You will have the option of printing all of your output or just the currently se-lected section. Be careful when printing! Each time you run a command, the output is added to the end of your previous output. Thus, you could be printing a very large output file containing information you may not want or need.

One way to ensure that your **output window** contains only the results of the current command is to create a new **output window** just before running the command. To do this, click *File*, then *New*, then *Output*. All your subsequent commands will go into your new **output window**.

Practice Exercise

Load the sample data file you created earlier (SAMPLE.sav). Run the *Descriptives* command for the variable GRADE and print the output. Your output should look like the example on page 7. Next, select the **data window** and print it.

Section 1.7   Modifying Data Files

Once you have created a data file, it is really quite simple to add additional cases (rows/participants) or additional variables (columns). Consider Example 1.7.1.

Example 1.7.1

Two more students provide you with surveys. Their information is:

Response Sheet 3
ID:	8734	
Day of class:	_____ MWF	X TTh
Class time:	X Morning	_____ Afternoon
Are you a morning person?	_____ Yes	X No
Final grade in class:	80%	
Do you work outside school?	_____ Full-time	_____ Part-time
	X No	

Response Sheet 4
ID:	1909	
Day of class:	X MWF	_____ TTH
Class time:	X Morning	_____ Afternoon
Are you a morning person?	X Yes	_____ No
Final grade in class:	73%	
Do you work outside school?	_____ Full-time	X Part-time
	_____ No	

To add these data, simply place two additional rows in the *Data View* window (after loading your sample data). Notice that as new participants are added, the row numbers become bold. When done, the screen should look like the screenshot here.

	ID	DAY	TIME	MORNING	GRADE	WORK	var	
1	4593.00	Tue/Thu	afternoon	No	85.00	No		
2	1901.00	Mon/Wed/	morning	Yes	83.00	Part-Time		
3	8734.00	Tue/Thu	morning	No	80.00	No		
4	1909.00	Mon/Wed/	morning	Yes	73.00	Part-Time		
5								
6								

sample.sav [DataSet1] - SPSS Data Editor — File Edit View Data Transform Analyze Graphs Utilities Window Help — 5 : WORK — Visible: 6 of — Data View / Variable View / — SPSS Processor is ready

New variables can also be added. For example, if the first two participants were given special training on time management, and the two new participants were not, the data file can be changed to reflect this additional information. The new variable could be called TRAINING (whether or not the participant received training), and it would be coded so that 0 = No and 1 = Yes. Thus, the first two participants would be assigned a "1" and the last two participants a "0." To do this, switch to the *Variable View* window, then add the TRAINING variable to the bottom of the list. Then switch back to the *Data View* window to update the data.

	ID	DAY	TIME	MORNING	GRADE	WORK	TRAINING	
1	4593.00	Tue/Thu	afternoon	No	85.00	No	Yes	
2	1901.00	Mon/Wed/	morning	Yes	83.00	Part-Time	Yes	
3	8734.00	Tue/Thu	morning	No	80.00	No	No	
4	1909.00	Mon/Wed/	morning	Yes	73.00	Part-Time	No	
5								
6								

sample.sav [DataSet1] - SPSS Data Editor — File Edit View Data Transform Analyze Graphs Utilities Window Help — 4 : TRAINING — 0 — Visible: 7 of — Data View / Variable View / — SPSS Processor is ready

Adding data and adding variables are just logical extensions of the procedures we used to originally create the data file. Save this new data file. We will be using it again later in the book.

Practice Exercise

Follow the example above (where TRAINING is the new variable). Make the modifications to your SAMPLE.sav data file and save it.

Chapter 2

Entering and Modifying Data

In Chapter 1, we learned how to create a simple data file, save it, perform a basic analysis, and examine the output. In this section, we will go into more detail about variables and data.

Section 2.1 Variables and Data Representation

In SPSS, variables are represented as columns in the data file. Participants are represented as rows. Thus, if we collect 4 pieces of information from 100 participants, we will have a data file with 4 columns and 100 rows.

Measurement Scales

There are four types of measurement scales: **nominal**, **ordinal**, **interval**, and **ratio**. While the measurement scale will determine which statistical technique is appropriate for a given set of data, SPSS generally does not discriminate. Thus, we start this section with this warning: If you ask it to, SPSS may conduct an analysis that is not appropriate for your data. For a more complete description of these four measurement scales, consult your statistics text or the glossary in Appendix C.

Newer versions of SPSS allow you to indicate which types of data you have when you define your variable. You do this using the *Measure* column. You can indicate Nominal, Ordinal, or Scale (SPSS does not distinguish between **interval** and **ratio** scales).

Look at the sample data file we created in Chapter 1. We calculated a **mean** for the variable GRADE. GRADE was measured on a **ratio scale**, and the **mean** is an acceptable summary statistic (assuming that the distribution is **normal**).

We could have had SPSS calculate a **mean** for the variable TIME instead of GRADE. If we did, we would get the output presented here.

The output indicates that the average TIME was 1.25. Remember that TIME was coded as an ordinal variable (1 = morning class, 2 = afternoon class). Thus, the **mean** is not an appropriate statistic for an **ordinal scale**, but SPSS calculated it anyway. The importance of considering the type of data cannot be overemphasized. Just because SPSS will compute a statistic for you does not mean that you should

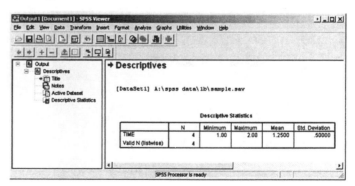

use it. Later in the text, when specific statistical procedures are discussed, the conditions under which they are appropriate will be addressed.

Missing Data

Often, participants do not provide complete data. For some students, you may have a pretest score but not a posttest score. Perhaps one student left one question blank on a survey, or perhaps she did not state her age. Missing data can weaken any analysis. Often,

q1	q2	total
2.00	2.00	4.00
3.00	1.00	4.00
4.00	3.00	7.00
2.00	.	.
1.00	2.00	3.00

a single missing question can eliminate a subject from all analyses.

If you have missing data in your data set, leave that cell blank. In the example to the left, the fourth subject did not complete Question 2. Note that the total score (which is calculated from both questions) is also blank because of the missing data for Question 2. SPSS represents missing data in the **data window** with a period (although you should not enter a period—just leave it blank).

Section 2.2   Transformation and Selection of Data

We often have more data in a data file than we want to include in a specific analysis. For example, our sample data file contains data from four participants, two of whom received special training and two of whom did not. If we wanted to conduct an analysis using only the two participants who did not receive the training, we would need to specify the appropriate subset.

Selecting a Subset

We can use the *Select Cases* command to specify a subset of our data. The *Select Cases* command is located under the *Data* menu. When you select this command, the **dialog box** below will appear.

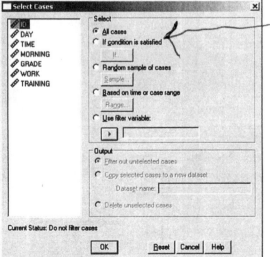

You can specify which cases (participants) you want to select by using the selection criteria, which appear on the right side of the Select Cases **dialog box**.

By default, *All cases* will be selected. The most common way to select a subset is to click *If condition is satisfied*, then click on the button labeled *If.* This will bring up a new **dialog box** that allows you to indicate which cases you would like to use.

You can enter the logic used to select the subset in the upper section. If the logical statement is true for a given case, then that case will be selected. If the logical statement is false, that case will not be selected. For example, you can select all cases that were coded as Mon/Wed/Fri by entering the formula DAY = 1 in the upper-

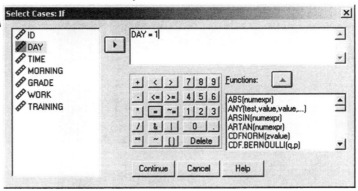

right part of the window. If DAY is 1, then the statement will be true, and SPSS will select the case. If DAY is anything other than 1, the statement will be false, and the case will not be selected. Once you have entered the logical statement, click *Continue* to return to the Select Cases **dialog box.** Then, click *OK* to return to the **data window.**

After you have selected the cases, the **data window** will change slightly. The cases that were not selected will be marked with a diagonal line through the case number. For example, for our sample data, the first and third cases are not selected. Only the second and fourth cases are selected for this subset.

	ID	DAY	TIME	MORNING	GRADE	WORK	TRAINING	FILTER_$
1	4593.00	Tue/Thu	afternoon	No	85.00	No	Yes	Not Selected
2	1901.00	Mon/Wed/	morning	Yes	83.00	Part-Time	Yes	Selected
3	8734.00	Tue/Thu	morning	No	80.00	No	No	Not Selected
4	1909.00	Mon/Wed/	morning	Yes	73.00	Part-Time	No	Selected
5								

An additional variable will also be created in your data file. The new variable is called FILTER_$ and indicates whether a case was selected or not.

If we calculate a **mean** GRADE using the subset we just selected, we will receive the output at right. Notice that we now have a **mean** of 78.00 with a sample size (*N*) of 2 instead of 4.

Descriptive Statistics

	N	Minimum	Maximum	Mean	Std. Deviation
GRADE	2	73.00	83.00	78.0000	7.0711
Valid N (listwise)	2				

Be careful when you select subsets. *The subset remains in effect until you run the command again and select all cases.* You can tell if you have a subset selected because the bottom of the **data window** will indicate that a filter is on. In addition, when you examine your output, *N* will be less than the total number of records in your data set if a subset is selected. The diagonal lines through some cases will also be evident when a subset is selected. Be careful not to save your data file with a subset selected, as this can cause considerable confusion later.

Computing a New Variable

SPSS can also be used to compute a new variable or manipulate your existing variables. To illustrate this, we will create a new data file. This file will contain data for four participants and three variables (Q1, Q2, and Q3). The variables represent the number of points each participant received on three different questions. Now enter

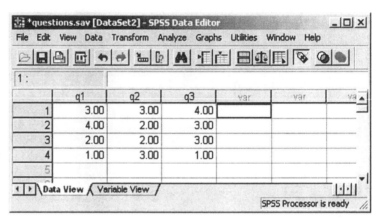

the data shown on the screen to the right. When done, save this data file as "QUESTIONS.sav." We will be using it again in later chapters.

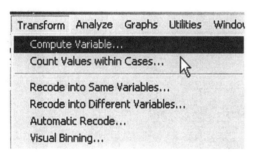

Now you will calculate the total score for each subject. We could do this manually, but if the data file were large, or if there were a lot of questions, this would take a long time. It is more efficient (and more accurate) to have SPSS compute the totals for you. To do this, click *Transform* and then click *Compute Variable*.

After clicking the *Compute Variable* command, we get the **dialog box** at right.

The blank field marked *Target Variable* is where we enter the name of the new variable we want to create. In this example, we are creating a variable called TOTAL, so type the word "total."

Notice that there is an equals sign between the *Target Variable* blank and the *Numeric Expression* blank. These two blank areas are the

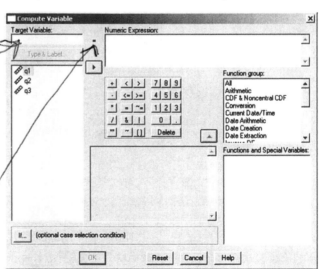

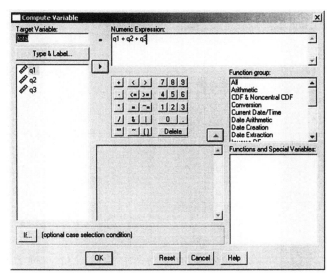

two sides of an equation that SPSS will calculate. For example, total = q1 + q2 + q3 is the equation that is entered in the sample presented here (screenshot at left). Note that it is possible to create any equation here simply by using the number and operational keypad at the bottom of the **dialog box**. When we click *OK*, SPSS will create a new variable called TOTAL and make it equal to the sum of the three questions.

Save your data file again so that the new variable will be available for future sessions.

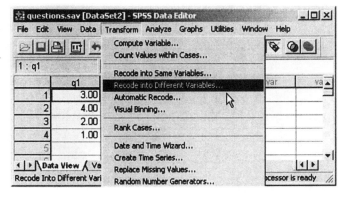

Recoding a Variable—Different Variable

SPSS can create a new variable based upon data from another variable. Say we want to split our participants on the basis of their total score. We want to create a variable called GROUP, which is coded 1 if the total score is low (less than or equal to 8) or 2 if the total score is high (9 or larger). To do this, we click *Transform*, then *Recode into Different Variables*.

This will bring up the Recode into Different Variables **dialog box** shown here. Transfer the variable TOTAL to the middle blank. Type "group" in the Name field under Output Variable. Click *Change*, and the middle blank will show that TOTAL is becoming GROUP, as shown below.

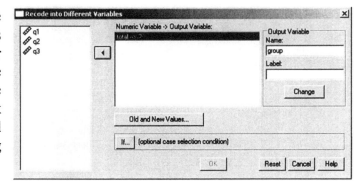

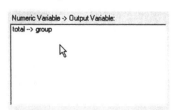

To help keep track of variables that have been recoded, it's a good idea to open the Variable View and enter "Recoded" in the *Label* column in the TOTAL row. This is especially useful with large datasets which may include many recoded variables.

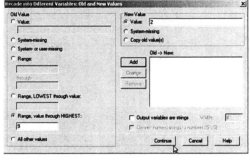

Click *Old* and *New Values*. This will bring up the Recode **dialog box**. In this example, we have entered a 9 in the *Range, value through HIGHEST* field and a 2 in the *Value* field under *New Value*. When we click *Add*, the blank on the right displays the recoding formula. Now enter an 8 on the left in the *Range, LOWEST through value* blank and a 1 in the *Value* field under *New Value*. Click *Add*, then *Continue*. Click *OK*. You will be redirected to the **data window**. A new variable (GROUP) will have been added and coded as 1 or 2, based on TOTAL.

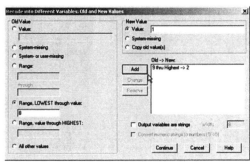

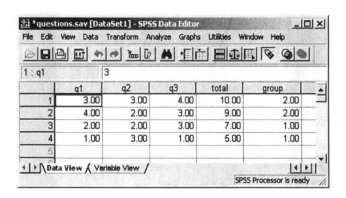

Chapter 3

Descriptive Statistics

In Chapter 2, we discussed many of the options available in SPSS for dealing with data. Now we will discuss ways to summarize our data. The procedures used to describe and summarize data are called **descriptive statistics**.

Section 3.1   Frequency Distributions and Percentile Ranks for a Single Variable

Description

The *Frequencies* command produces frequency distributions for the specified variables. The output includes the number of occurrences, percentages, valid percentages, and cumulative percentages. The valid percentages and the cumulative percentages comprise only the data that are not designated as missing.

The *Frequencies* command is useful for describing samples where the **mean** is not useful (e.g., **nominal** or **ordinal** scales). It is also useful as a method of getting the feel of your data. It provides more information than just a **mean** and **standard deviation** and can be useful in determining **skew** and identifying **outliers**. A special feature of the command is its ability to determine **percentile ranks**.

Assumptions

Cumulative percentages and **percentiles** are valid only for data that are measured on at least an **ordinal scale**. Because the output contains one line for each value of a variable, this command works best on variables with a relatively small number of values.

Drawing Conclusions

The *Frequencies* command produces output that indicates both the number of cases in the sample of a particular value and the percentage of cases with that value. Thus, conclusions drawn should relate only to describing the numbers or percentages of cases in the sample. If the data are at least ordinal in nature, conclusions regarding the cumulative percentage and/or **percentiles** can be drawn.

SPSS Data Format

The SPSS data file for obtaining frequency distributions requires only one variable, and that variable can be of any type.

Creating a Frequency Distribution

To run the *Frequencies* command, click *Analyze*, then *Descriptive Statistics*, then *Frequencies*. (This example uses the CARS.sav data file that comes with SPSS. It is typically located at <C:\Program Files\SPSS\Cars.sav>.)

This will bring up the main **dialog box**. Transfer the variable for which you would like a frequency distribution into the

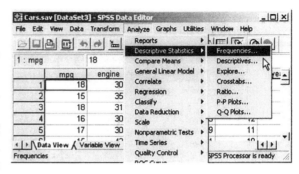

Variable(s) blank to the right. Be sure that the *Display frequency tables* option is checked. Click *OK* to receive your output.

Note that the **dialog boxes** in newer versions of SPSS show both the type of variable (the icon immediately left of the variable name) and the variable labels if they are entered. Thus, the variable YEAR shows up in the **dialog box** as *Model Year (modulo 10)*.

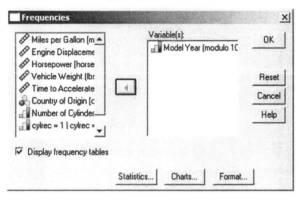

Output for a Frequency Distribution

The output consists of two sections. The first section indicates the number of re-cords with **valid data** for each variable selected. Records with a blank score are listed as missing. In this example, the data file contained 406 records. Notice that the variable label is Model Year (modulo 100).

Statistics

Model Year (modulo 100)

N	Valid	405
	Missing	1

The second section of the output contains a cumulative frequency distribution for each variable selected. At the top of the section, the variable label is given. The output itself consists of five columns. The first column lists the values of the variable in sorted order. There is a row for each value of your variable, and additional rows are added at the bottom for the Total and Missing data. The second column gives the frequency of each value, including missing values. The third column gives the percentage of all records (including records with missing data) for each value. The fourth column, labeled *Valid Percent*, gives the percentage of records (without including records with missing data) for each value. If there were any missing values, these values would be larger than the values in column three because the total

Model Year (modulo 100)

		Frequency	Percent	Valid Percent	Cumulative Percent
Valid	70	34	8.4	8.4	8.4
	71	29	7.1	7.2	15.6
	72	28	6.9	6.9	22.5
	73	40	9.9	9.9	32.3
	74	27	6.7	6.7	39.0
	75	30	7.4	7.4	46.4
	76	34	8.4	8.4	54.8
	77	28	6.9	6.9	61.7
	78	36	8.9	8.9	70.6
	79	29	7.1	7.2	77.8
	80	29	7.1	7.2	84.9
	81	30	7.4	7.4	92.3
	82	31	7.6	7.7	100.0
	Total	405	99.8	100.0	
Missing	0 (Missing)	1	.2		
Total		406	100.0		

number of records would have been reduced by the number of records with missing values. The final column gives cumulative percentages. Cumulative percentages indicate the percentage of records with a score equal to or smaller than the current value. Thus, the last value is always 100%. These values are equivalent to **percentile ranks** for the values listed.

Determining Percentile Ranks

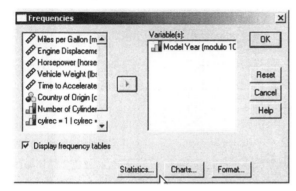

The *Frequencies* command can be used to provide a number of **descriptive statistics**, as well as a variety of percentile values (including **quartiles**, cut points, and scores corresponding to a specific **percentile rank**).

To obtain either the descriptive or percentile functions of the *Frequencies* command, click the *Statistics* button at the bottom of the main **dialog box**. Note that the *Central Tendency* and *Dispersion* sections of this box are useful for calculating values, such as the **Median** or **Mode**, which cannot be calculated with the *Descriptives* command (see Section 3.3).

This brings up the Frequencies: Statistics **dialog box**. Check any additional desired statistic by clicking on the blank next to it. For **percentiles**, enter the desired **percentile rank** in the blank to the right of the *Percentile(s)* label. Then, click *Add* to add it to the list of **percentiles** requested. Once you have selected all your required statistics, click *Continue* to return to the main **dialog box**. Click *OK*.

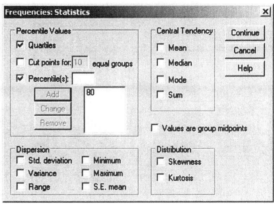

Output for Percentile Ranks

The Statistics **dialog box** adds on to the previous output from the *Frequencies* command. The new section of the output is shown at left.

The output contains a row for each piece of information you requested. In the example above, we checked *Quartiles* and asked for the 80th **percentile**. Thus, the output contains rows for the 25th, 50th, 75th, and 80th **percentiles**.

Statistics

Model Year (modulo 100)

N	Valid	405
	Missing	1
Percentiles	25	73.00
	50	76.00
	75	79.00
	80	80.00

Practice Exercise

Using Practice Data Set 1 in Appendix B, create a frequency distribution table for the mathematics skills scores. Determine the mathematics skills score at which the 60th percentile lies.

Section 3.2   Frequency Distributions and Percentile Ranks for Multiple Variables

Description

The *Crosstabs* command produces frequency distributions for multiple variables. The output includes the number of occurrences of each combination of **levels** of each variable. It is possible to have the command give percentages for any or all variables.

The *Crosstabs* command is useful for describing samples where the **mean** is not useful (e.g., **nominal** or **ordinal scales**). It is also useful as a method for getting a feel for your data.

Assumptions

Because the output contains a row or column for each value of a variable, this command works best on variables with a relatively small number of values.

SPSS Data Format

The SPSS data file for the *Crosstabs* command requires two or more variables. Those variables can be of any type.

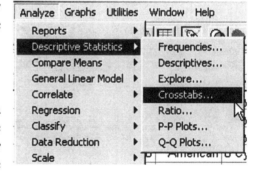

Running the Crosstabs Command

This example uses the SAMPLE.sav data file, which you created in Chapter 1. To run the procedure, click *Analyze*, then *Descriptive Statistics*, then *Crosstabs*. This will bring up the main Crosstabs **dialog box**, below.

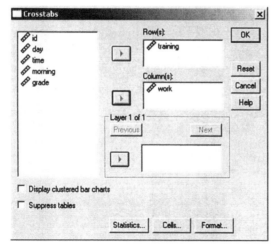

The **dialog box** initially lists all variables on the left and contains two blanks labeled *Row(s)* and *Column(s)*. Enter one variable (TRAINING) in the *Row(s)* box. Enter the second (WORK) in the *Column(s)* box. To analyze more than two variables, you would enter the third, fourth, etc., in the unlabeled area (just under the *Layer* indicator).

The *Cells* button allows you to specify percentages and other information to be generated for each combination of values. Click *Cells*, and you will get the box at right.

For the example presented here, check *Row, Column,* and *Total* percentages. Then click *Continue*. This will return you to the Crosstabs **dialog box**. Click *OK* to run the analysis.

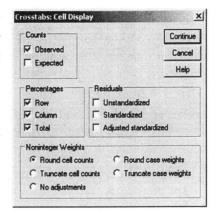

TRAINING ' WORK Crosstabulation

			WORK		Total
			No	Part-Time	
TRAINING	Yes	Count	1	1	2
		% within TRAINING	50.0%	50.0%	100.0%
		% within WORK	50.0%	50.0%	50.0%
		% of Total	25.0%	25.0%	50.0%
	No	Count	1	1	2
		% within TRAINING	50.0%	50.0%	100.0%
		% within WORK	50.0%	50.0%	50.0%
		% of Total	25.0%	25.0%	50.0%
Total		Count	2	2	4
		% within TRAINING	50.0%	50.0%	100.0%
		% within WORK	100.0%	100.0%	100.0%
		% of Total	50.0%	50.0%	100.0%

Interpreting Crosstabs Output

The output consists of a contingency table. Each level of WORK is given a column. Each level of TRAINING is given a row. In addition, a row is added for total, and a column is added for total.

Each cell contains the number of participants (e.g., one participant received no training and does not work; two participants received no training, regardless of employment status).

The percentages for each cell are also shown. Row percentages add up to 100% horizontally. Column percentages add up to 100% vertically. For example, of all the individuals who had no training, 50% did not work and 50% worked part-time (using the "% within TRAINING" row). Of the individuals who did not work, 50% had no training and 50% had training (using the "% within work" row).

Practice Exercise

Using Practice Data Set 1 in Appendix B, create a contingency table using the *Crosstabs* command. Determine the number of participants in each combination of the variables SEX and MARITAL. What percentage of participants is married? What percentage of participants is male and married?

Section 3.3   Measures of Central Tendency and Measures of Dispersion for a Single Group

Description

Measures of central tendency are values that represent a typical member of the sample or population. The three primary types are the **mean, median**, and **mode**. Measures of dispersion tell you the variability of your scores. The primary types are the **range** and the **standard deviation**. Together, a measure of central tendency and a measure of dispersion provide a great deal of information about the entire data set.

We will discuss these measures of central tendency and measures of dispersion in the context of the *Descriptives* command. Note that many of these statistics can also be calculated with several other commands (e.g., the *Frequencies* or *Compare Means* commands are required to compute the **mode** or **median**—the *Statistics* option for the *Frequencies* command is shown here).

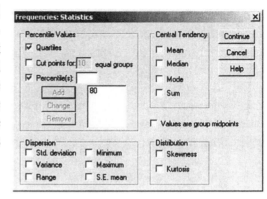

Assumptions

Each measure of central tendency and measure of dispersion has different assumptions associated with it. The **mean** is the most powerful measure of central tendency, and it has the most assumptions. For example, to calculate a **mean**, the data must be measured on an **interval** or **ratio scale**. In addition, the distribution should be normally distributed or, at least, not highly skewed. The **median** requires at least **ordinal** data. Because the **median** indicates only the middle score (when scores are arranged in order), there are no assumptions about the shape of the distribution. The **mode** is the weakest measure of central tendency. There are no assumptions for the **mode**.

The **standard deviation** is the most powerful measure of dispersion, but it, too, has several requirements. It is a mathematical transformation of the **variance** (the **standard deviation** is the square root of the **variance**). Thus, if one is appropriate, the other is also. The **standard deviation** requires data measured on an **interval** or **ratio scale**. In addition, the distribution should be normal. The **range** is the weakest measure of dispersion. To calculate a **range**, the variable must be at least **ordinal**. For **nominal scale** data, the entire frequency distribution should be presented as a measure of dispersion.

Drawing Conclusions

A measure of central tendency should be accompanied by a measure of dispersion. Thus, when reporting a **mean**, you should also report a **standard deviation**. When presenting a **median**, you should also state the **range** or interquartile **range**.

SPSS Data Format

Only one variable is required.

Running the Command

The *Descriptives* command will be the command you will most likely use for obtaining measures of central tendency and measures of dispersion. This example uses the SAMPLE.sav data file we have used in the previous chapters.

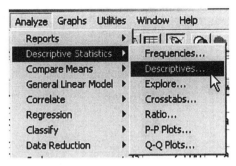

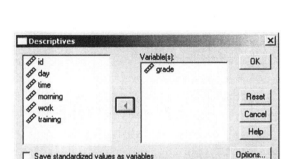

To run the command, click *Analyze*, then *Descriptive Statistics*, then *Descriptives*. This will bring up the main **dialog box** for the *Descriptives* command. Any variables you would like information about can be placed in the right blank by double-clicking them or by selecting them, then clicking on the arrow.

By default, you will receive the *N* (number of cases/participants), the minimum value, the maximum value, the **mean**, and the **standard deviation**. Note that some of these may not be appropriate for the type of data you have selected.

If you would like to change the default statistics that are given, click *Options* in the main **dialog box**. You will be given the Options **dialog box** presented here.

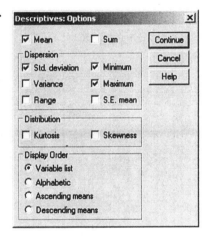

Reading the Output

The output for the *Descriptives* command is quite straightforward. Each type of output requested is presented in a column, and each variable is given in a row. The output presented here is for the sample data file. It shows that we have one variable (GRADE) and that we obtained the *N*, minimum, maximum, **mean**, and **standard deviation** for this variable.

Descriptive Statistics

	N	Minimum	Maximum	Mean	Std. Deviation
grade	4	73.00	85.00	80.2500	5.25198
Valid N (listwise)	4				

Practice Exercise

Using Practice Data Set 1 in Appendix B, obtain the **descriptive statistics** for the age of the participants. What is the **mean**? The **median**? The **mode**? What is the **standard deviation**? Minimum? Maximum? The **range**?

Section 3.4   Measures of Central Tendency and Measures of Dispersion for Multiple Groups

Description

The measures of central tendency discussed earlier are often needed not only for the entire data set, but also for several subsets. One way to obtain these values for subsets would be to use the data-selection techniques discussed in Chapter 2 and apply the *Descriptives* command to each subset. An easier way to perform this task is to use the *Means* command. The *Means* command is designed to provide **descriptive statistics** for subsets of your data.

Assumptions

The assumptions discussed in the section on Measures of Central Tendency and Measures of Dispersion for a Single Group (Section 3.3) also apply to multiple groups.

Drawing Conclusions

A measure of central tendency should be accompanied by a measure of dispersion. Thus, when giving a **mean**, you should also report a **standard deviation**. When presenting a **median**, you should also state the **range** or interquartile **range**.

SPSS Data Format

Two variables in the SPSS data file are required. One represents the **dependent variable** and will be the variable for which you receive the **descriptive statistics**. The other is the **independent variable** and will be used in creating the subsets. Note that while SPSS calls this variable an **independent variable**, it may not meet the strict criteria that define a true **independent variable** (e.g., treatment manipulation). Thus, some SPSS procedures refer to it as the **grouping variable**.

Running the Command

This example uses the SAMPLE.sav data file you created in Chapter 1. The *Means* command is run by clicking *Analyze*, then *Compare Means*, then *Means*.

This will bring up the main **dialog box** for the *Means* command. Place the selected variable in the blank field labeled *Dependent List*.

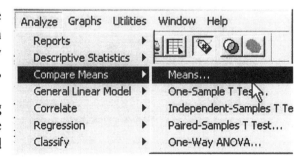

24

Place the **grouping variable** in the box labeled *Independent List*. In this example, through use of the SAMPLE.sav data file, measures of central tendency and measures of dispersion for the variable GRADE will be given for each level of the variable MORNING.

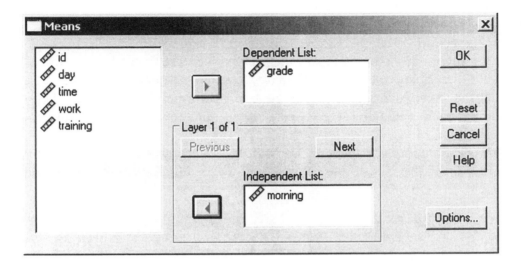

By default, the **mean**, number of cases, and **standard deviation** are given. If you would like additional measures, click *Options* and you will be presented with the **dialog box** at right. You can opt to include any number of measures.

Reading the Output

The output for the *Means* command is split into two sections. The first section, called a **case processing summary**, gives information about the data used. In our sample data file, there are four students (cases), all of whom were included in the analysis.

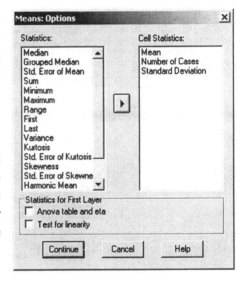

Case Processing Summary

	Cases					
	Included		Excluded		Total	
	N	Percent	N	Percent	N	Percent
grade * morning	4	100.0%	0	.0%	4	100.0%

The second section of the output is the report from the *Means* command.

This report lists the name of the **dependent variable** at the top (GRADE). Every **level** of the **independent variable** (MORNING) is

Report

GRADE

MORNING	Mean	N	Std. Deviation
No	82.5000	2	3.53553
Yes	78.0000	2	7.07107
Total	80.2500	4	5.25198

shown in a row in the table. In this example, the **levels** are 0 and 1, labeled No and Yes. Note that if a variable is labeled, the labels will be used instead of the raw values.

The summary statistics given in the report correspond to the data, where the **level** of the **independent variable** is equal to the row heading (e.g., No, Yes). Thus, two participants were included in each row.

An additional row is added, named Total. That row contains the combined data, and the values are the same as they would be if we had run the *Descriptives* command for the variable GRADE.

Extension to More Than One Independent Variable

If you have more than one **independent variable**, SPSS can break down the output even further. Rather than adding more variables to the *Independent List* section of the **dialog box**, you need to add them in a different layer. Note that SPSS indicates with which layer you are working.

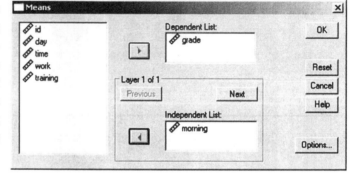

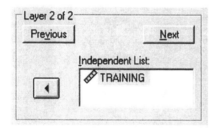

If you click *Next*, you will be presented with *Layer 2 of 2*, and you can select a second **independent variable** (e.g., TRAINING). Now, when you run the command (by clicking *OK*), you will be given summary statistics for the variable GRADE by each level of MORNING and TRAINING.

Your output will look like the output at right. You now have two main sections (No and Yes), along with the Total. Now, however, each main section is broken down into subsections (No, Yes, and Total).

The variable you used in Level 1 (MORNING) is the first one listed, and it defines the main sections. The variable you had in Level 2 (TRAINING) is listed sec-

Report

GRADE

MORNING	TRAINING	Mean	N	Std. Deviation
No	Yes	85.0000	1	.
	No	80.0000	1	.
	Total	82.5000	2	3.53553
Yes	Yes	83.0000	1	.
	No	73.0000	1	.
	Total	78.0000	2	7.07107
Total	Yes	84.0000	2	1.41421
	No	76.5000	2	4.94975
	Total	80.2500	4	5.25198

ond. Thus, the first row represents those participants who were not morning people and who received training. The second row represents participants who were not morning people and did not receive training. The third row represents the total for all participants who were not morning people.

Notice that **standard deviations** are not given for all of the rows. This is because there is only one participant per cell in this example. One problem with using many subsets is that it increases the number of participants required to obtain meaningful results. See a research design text or your instructor for more details.

Practice Exercise

Using Practice Data Set 1 in Appendix B, compute the **mean** and **standard deviation** of ages for each value of marital status. What is the average age of the married participants? The single participants? The divorced participants?

Section 3.5   Standard Scores

Description

Standard scores allow the comparison of different scales by transforming the scores into a common scale. The most common standard score is the *z*-score. A *z*-score is based on a **standard normal distribution** (e.g., a **mean** of 0 and a **standard deviation** of 1). A *z*-score, therefore, represents the number of **standard deviations** above or below the **mean** (e.g., a *z*-score of −1.5 represents a score 1½ **standard deviations** below the **mean**).

Assumptions

Z-scores are based on the **standard normal distribution**. Therefore, the distributions that are converted to *z*-scores should be normally distributed, and the scales should be either **interval** or **ratio**.

Drawing Conclusions

Conclusions based on *z*-scores consist of the number of **standard deviations** above or below the **mean**. For example, a student scores 85 on a mathematics exam in a class that has a **mean** of 70 and **standard deviation** of 5. The student's test score is 15 points above the class **mean** (85 − 70 = 15). The student's *z*-score is 3 because she scored 3 **standard deviations** above the **mean** (15 ÷ 5 = 3). If the same student scores 90 on a reading exam, with a class **mean** of 80 and a **standard deviation** of 10, the *z*-score will be 1.0 because she is one **standard deviation** above the **mean**. Thus, even though her raw score was higher on the reading test, she actually did better in relation to other students on the mathematics test because her *z*-score was higher on that test.

SPSS Data Format

Calculating *z*-scores requires only a single variable in SPSS. That variable must be numerical.

Running the Command

Computing *z*-scores is a component of the *Descriptives* command. To access it, click *Analyze*, then *Descriptive Statistics,* then *Descriptives.* This example uses the sample data file (SAMPLE.sav) created in Chapters 1 and 2.

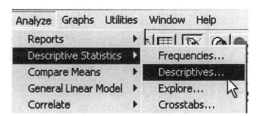

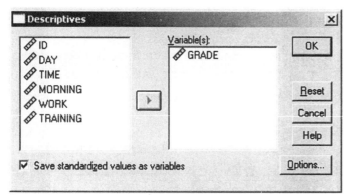

This will bring up the standard **dialog box** for the *Descriptives* command. Notice the checkbox in the bottom-left corner labeled *Save standardized values as variables*. Check this box and move the variable GRADE into the right-hand blank. Then click *OK* to complete the analysis. You will be presented with the standard output from the *Descriptives* command. Notice that the *z*-scores are not listed. They were inserted into the **data window** as a new variable.

Switch to the *Data View* window and examine your data file. Notice that a new variable, called ZGRADE, has been added. When you asked SPSS to save standardized values, it created a new variable with the same name as your old variable preceded by a Z. The *z*-score is computed for each case and placed in the new variable.

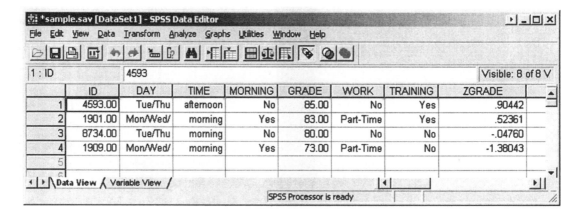

Reading the Output

After you conducted your analysis, the new variable was created. You can perform any number of subsequent analyses on the new variable.

Practice Exercise

Using Practice Data Set 2 in Appendix B, determine the *z*-score that corresponds to each employee's salary. Determine the **mean** *z*-scores for salaries of male employees and female employees. Determine the **mean** *z*-score for salaries of the total sample.

Chapter 4

Graphing Data

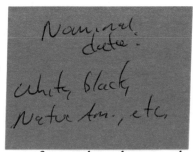

Nominal data: white, black, Native Am., etc.

Section 4.1   Graphing Basics

In addition to the frequency distributions, the measures of central tendency and measures of dispersion discussed in Chapter 3, graphing is a useful way to summarize, organize, and reduce your data. It has been said that a picture is worth a thousand words. In the case of complicated data sets, this is certainly true.

With Version 15.0 of SPSS, it is now possible to make publication-quality graphs using only SPSS. One important advantage of using SPSS to create your graphs instead of other software (e.g., Excel or SigmaPlot) is that the data have already been entered. Thus, duplication is eliminated, and the chance of making a transcription error is reduced.

Ratio Data: Has natural 0.

New SPSS Chart Builder

...hing examples, we will use a new set of data. Enter the data below by ...subject variables in the *Variable View* window: HEIGHT (in inches), ...ds), and SEX (1 = male, 2 = female). When you create the variables, designate HEIGHT and WEIGHT as *Scale* measures and SEX as a *Nominal* measure (in the far-right column of the *Variable View*). Switch to the *Data View* to enter the data values for the 16 participants. Now use the *Save As* command to save the file, naming it HEIGHT.sav.

Measure
Scale
Scale
Nominal

Interval Data: Temperature continuous data

HEIGHT	WEIGHT	SEX
66	150	1
69	155	1
73	160	1
72	160	1
68	150	1
63	140	1
74	165	1
70	150	1
66	110	2
64	100	2
60	95	2
67	110	2
64	105	2
63	100	2
67	110	2
65	105	2

either one or the other

because it changes up or down

Scale — up or down

Ay — = Ratio or ordinal

Make sure you have entered the data correctly by calculating a **mean** for each of the three variables (click *Analyze*, then *Descriptive Statistics*, then *Descriptives*). Compare your results with those in the table below.

Descriptive Statistics

	N	Minimum	Maximum	Mean	Std. Deviation
HEIGHT	16	60.00	74.00	66.9375	3.9067
WEIGHT	16	95.00	165.00	129.0625	26.3451
SEX	16	1.00	2.00	1.5000	.5164
Valid N (listwise)	16				

Chart Builder Basics

Make sure that the HEIGHT.sav data file you created above is open. In order to use the chart builder, you must have a data file open.

New with Version 15.0 of SPSS is the *Chart Builder* command. This command is accessed using *Graphs*, then *Chart Builder* in the submenu. This is a very versatile new command that can make graphs of excellent quality.

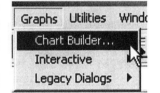

When you first run the *Chart Builder* command, you will probably be presented with the following **dialog box**:

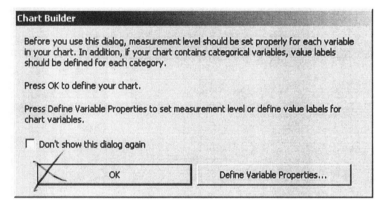

This **dialog box** is asking you to ensure that your variables are properly defined. Refer to Sections 1.3 and 2.1 if you had difficulty defining the variables used in creating the dataset for this example, or to refresh your knowledge of this topic. Click *OK*.

The Chart Builder allows you to make any kind of graph that is normally used in publication or presentation, and much of it is beyond the scope of this text. This text, however, will go over the basics of the Chart Builder so that you can understand its mechanics.

On the left side of the *Chart Builder* window are the four main tabs that let you control the graphs you are making. The first one is the *Gallery* tab. The *Gallery* tab allows you to choose the basic format of your graph.

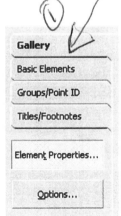

For example, the screenshot here shows the different kinds of bar charts that the Chart Builder can create.

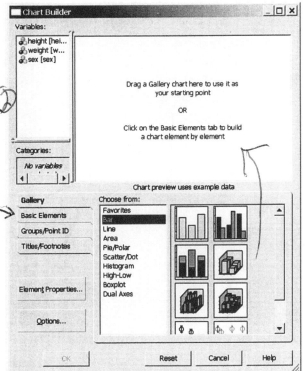

After you have selected the basic form of graph that you want using the *Gallery* tab, you simply drag the image  from the bottom right of the window up to the main window at the top (where it reads, "Drag a Gallery chart here to use it as your starting point").

Alternatively, you can use the *Basic Elements* tab to drag a coordinate system (labeled *Choose Axes*) to the top window, then drag variables and elements into the window.

The other tabs (*Groups/Point ID* and *Titles/Footnotes*) can be used for adding other standard elements to your graphs.

The examples in this text will cover some of the basic types of graphs you can make with the Chart Builder. After a little experimentation on your own, once you have mastered the examples in the chapter, you will soon gain a full understanding of the Chart Builder.

Section 4.3   Bar Charts, Pie Charts, and Histograms

Description

Bar charts, pie charts, and histograms represent the number of times each score occurs through the varying heights of bars or sizes of pie pieces. They are graphical representations of the frequency distributions discussed in Chapter 3.

Drawing Conclusions

The *Frequencies* command produces output that indicates both the number of cases in the sample with a particular value and the percentage of cases with that value. Thus, conclusions drawn should relate only to describing the numbers or percentages for the sample. If the data are at least **ordinal** in nature, conclusions regarding the cumulative percentages and/or **percentiles** can also be drawn.

SPSS Data Format

You need only one variable to use this command.

Running the Command

The *Frequencies* command will produce graphical frequency distributions. Click *Analyze*, then *Descriptive Statistics,* then *Frequencies.* You will be presented with the main **dialog box** for the *Frequencies* command, where you can enter the variables for which you would like to create graphs or charts. (See Chapter 3 for other options with this command.)

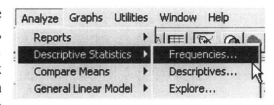

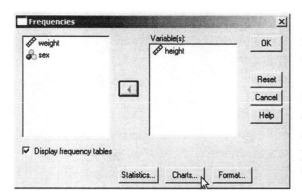

Click the *Charts* button at the bottom to produce frequency distributions. This will give you the Charts **dialog box**.

There are three types of charts available with this command: *Bar charts*, *Pie charts*, and *Histograms*. For each type, the *Y* axis can be either a frequency count or a percentage (selected with the *Chart Values* option).

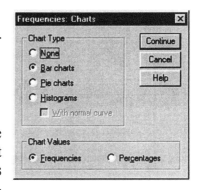

You will receive the charts for any variables selected in the main *Frequencies* command **dialog box**.

Output

The bar chart consists of a *Y* axis, representing the frequency, and an *X* axis, representing each score. Note that the only values represented on the *X* axis are those values with nonzero frequencies (61, 62, and 71 are not represented).

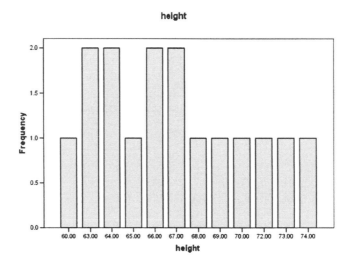

height

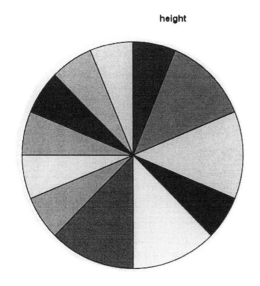

■	60.00
▨	63.00
□	64.00
■	65.00
□	66.00
■	67.00
▨	68.00
□	69.00
▨	70.00
■	72.00
▨	73.00
□	74.00

The pie chart shows the percentage of the whole that is represented by each value.

The *Histogram* command creates a grouped frequency distribution. The **range** of scores is split into evenly spaced groups. The midpoint of each group is plotted on the *X* axis, and the *Y* axis represents the number of scores for each group.

If you select *With Normal Curve*, a normal curve will be superimposed over the distribution. This is very useful in determining if the distribution you have is approximately normal. The distribution represented here is clearly not normal due to the asymmetry of the values.

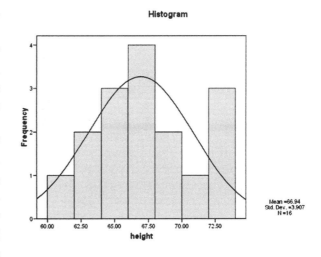

Histogram

Mean =66.94
Std. Dev. =3.907
N =16

Practice Exercise

Use Practice Data Set 1 in Appendix B. After you have entered the data, construct a histogram that represents the mathematics skills scores and displays a normal curve, and a bar chart that represents the frequencies for the variable AGE.

Section 4.4 Scatterplots

Description

Scatterplots (also called scattergrams or scatter diagrams) display two values for each case with a mark on the graph. The *X* axis represents the value for one variable. The *Y* axis represents the value for the second variable.

Assumptions

Both variables should be **interval** or **ratio scales**. If **nominal** or **ordinal** data are used, be cautious about your interpretation of the scattergram.

SPSS Data Format

You need two variables to perform this command.

Running the Command

You can produce scatterplots by clicking *Graphs*, then *Chart Builder*. (Note: You can also use the *Legacy Dialogs*. For this method, please see Appendix F.)

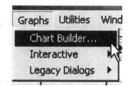

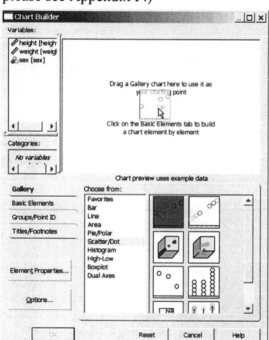

In *Gallery Choose from:* select *Scatter/Dot*. Then drag the *Simple Scatter* icon (top left) up to the main chart area as shown in the screenshot at left. Disregard the *Element Properties* window that pops up by choosing *Close*.

Next, drag the HEIGHT variable to the *X-Axis* area, and the WEIGHT variable to the *Y-Axis* area (remember that standard graphing conventions indicate that **dependent variables** should be *Y* and **independent variables** should be *X*. This would mean that we are trying to predict weights from heights). At this point, your screen should look like the example below. Note that your actual data are *not* shown—just a set of dummy values.

Click *OK*. You should get your new graph (next page) as Output.

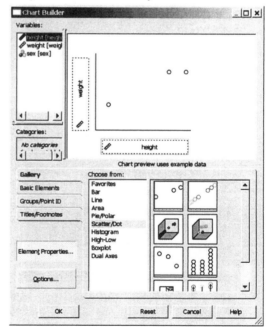

Output

The output will consist of a mark for each participant at the appropriate *X* and *Y* **levels**.

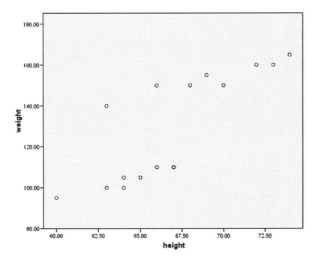

Adding a Third Variable

Even though the scatterplot is a two-dimensional graph, it can plot a third variable. To make it do so, select the *Groups/Point ID* tab in the Chart Builder. Click the *Grouping/stacking variable* option. Again, disregard the *Element Properties* window that pops up. Next, drag the variable SEX into the upper-right corner where it indicates *Set Color*. When this is done, your screen should look like the image at right. If you are not able to drag the variable SEX, it may be because it is not identified as **nominal** or **ordinal** in the *Variable View* window.

Click *OK* to have SPSS produce the graph.

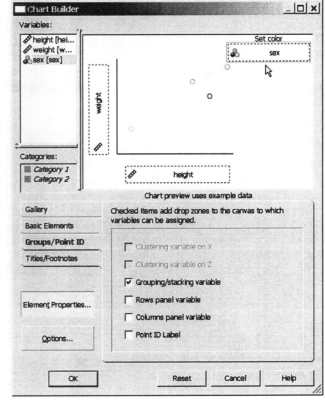

Now our output will have two different sets of marks. One set represents the male participants, and the second set represents the female participants. These two sets will appear in two different colors on your screen. You can use the SPSS chart editor (see Section 4.6) to make them different shapes, as shown in the example below.

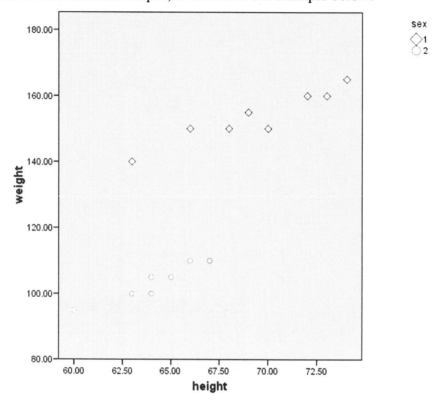

Practice Exercise

Use Practice Data Set 2 in Appendix B. Construct a scatterplot to examine the relationship between SALARY and EDUCATION.

Section 4.5   Advanced Bar Charts

Description

Bar charts can be produced with the *Frequencies* command (see Section 4.3). Sometimes, however, we are interested in a bar chart where the *Y* axis is not a frequency. To produce such a chart, we need to use the *Bar charts* command.

SPSS Data Format

You need at least two variables to perform this command. There are two basic kinds of bar charts—those for between-subjects designs and those for repeated-measures designs. Use the between-subjects method if one variable is the **independent variable** and the other is the **dependent variable**. Use the repeated-measures method if you have a **dependent variable** for each value of the **independent variable** (e.g., you would have three variables for a design with three values of the **independent variable**). This normally occurs when you make multiple observations over time.

This example uses the GRADES.sav data file, which will be created in Chapter 6. Please see Section 6.4 for the data if you would like to follow along.

Running the Command

Open the Chart Builder by clicking *Graphs*, then *Chart Builder*. In the *Gallery* tab, select *Bar*. If you had only one **independent variable**, you would select the Simple Bar Chart example (top left corner). If you have more than one **independent variable**

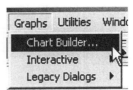

(as in this example), select the Clustered Bar Chart example from the middle of the top row.

Drag the example to the top working area. Once you do, the working area should look like the screenshot below. (Note that you will need to open the data file you would like to graph in order to run this command.)

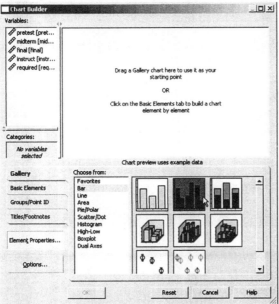

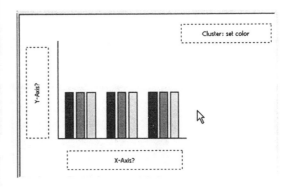

If you are using a repeated-measures design like our example here using GRADES.sav from Chapter 6 (three different variables representing the *Y* values that we want), you need to select all three variables (you can <Ctrl>-click them to select multiple variables) and then drag all three variable names to the *Y-Axis* area. When you do, you will be given the warning message above. Click *OK*.

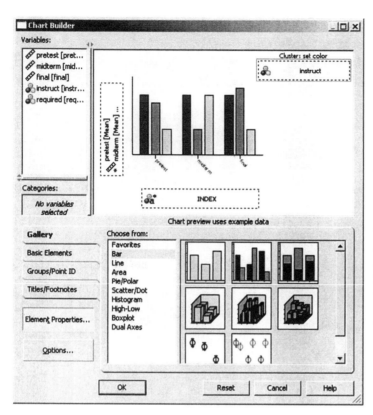

Next, you will need to drag the INSTRUCT variable to the top right in the *Cluster: set color* area (see screenshot at left).

Note: The Chart Builder pays attention to the types of variables that you ask it to graph. If you are getting error messages or unusual results, be sure that your categorical variables are properly designated as Nominal in the *Variable View* tab (See Chapter 2, Section 2.1).

Output

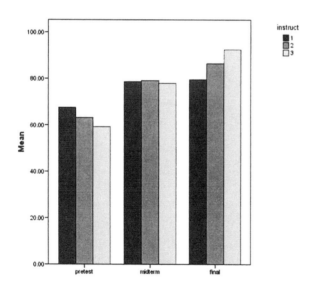

Practice Exercise

Use Practice Data Set 1 in Appendix B. Construct a clustered bar graph examining the relationship between MATHEMATICS SKILLS scores (as the **dependent variable**) and MARITAL STATUS and SEX (as **independent variables**). Make sure you classify both SEX and MARITAL STATUS as nominal variables.

Section 4.6   Editing SPSS Graphs

Whatever command you use to create your graph, you will probably want to do some editing to make it appear exactly as you want it to look. In SPSS, you do this in much the same way that you edit graphs in other software programs (e.g., Excel). After your graph is made, in the **output window**, select your graph (this will create handles around the outside of the entire object) and right-click. Then, click *SPSS Chart Object*, and click *Open*. Alternatively, you can double-click on the graph to open it for editing.

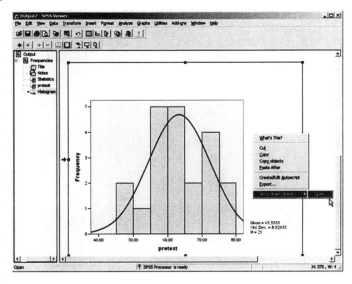

When you open the graph, the *Chart Editor* window and the corresponding *Properties* window will appear.

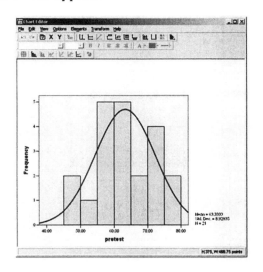
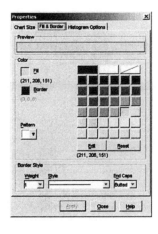

Once *Chart Editor* is open, you can easily edit each element of the graph. To select an element, just click on the relevant spot on the graph. For example, if you have added a title to your graph ("Histogram" in the example that follows), you may select the element representing the title of the graph by clicking anywhere on the title.

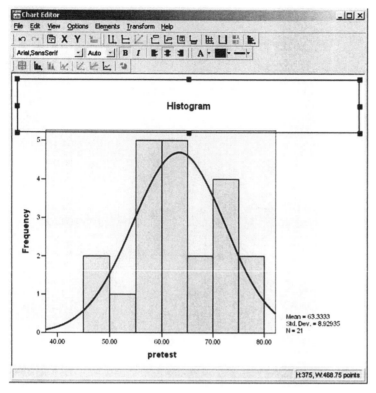

Once you have selected an element, you can tell whether the correct element is selected because it will have handles around it.

If the item you have selected is a text element (e.g., the title of the graph), a cursor will be present and you can edit the text as you would in a word processing program. If you would like to change another attribute of the element (e.g., the color or font size), use the Properties box. (Text properties are shown below.)

With a little practice, you can make excellent graphs using SPSS. Once your graph is formatted the way you want it, simply select *File*, *Save*, then *Close*.

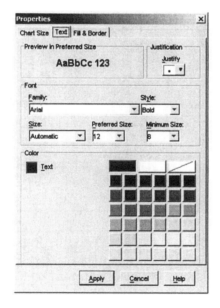

Chapter 5

Prediction and Association

Section 5.1 Pearson Correlation Coefficient

Description

The Pearson correlation coefficient (sometimes called the Pearson product-moment correlation coefficient or simply the Pearson *r*) determines the strength of the linear relationship between two variables.

Assumptions

Both variables should be measured on **interval** or **ratio scales** (or a **dichotomous** nominal variable). If a relationship exists between them, that relationship should be linear. Because the Pearson correlation coefficient is computed with *z*-scores, both variables should also be normally distributed. If your data do not meet these assumptions, consider using the Spearman *rho* correlation coefficient instead.

SPSS Data Format

Two variables are required in your SPSS data file. Each subject must have data for both variables.

Running the Command

To select the Pearson correlation coefficient, click *Analyze*, then *Correlate*, then *Bivariate* (bivariate refers to two variables). This will bring up the Bivariate Correlations **dialog box**. This example uses the HEIGHT.sav data file entered at the start of Chapter 4.

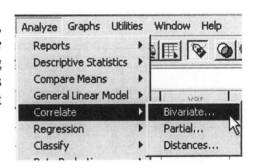

Move at least two variables from the box at left into the box at right by using the transfer arrow (or by double-clicking each variable). Make sure that a check is in the *Pearson* box under *Correlation Coefficients*. It is acceptable to move more than two variables.

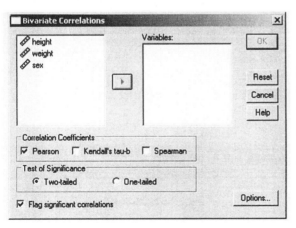

41

For our example, we will move all three variables over and click *OK*.

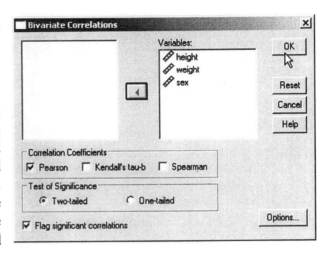

Reading the Output

The output consists of a **correlation matrix**. Every variable you entered in the command is represented as both a row and a column. We entered three variables in our command. Therefore, we have a 3 × 3 table. There are also three rows in each cell—the correlation, the **significance** level, and the *N*. If a correlation is significant at less than the .05 level, a single * will appear next to the correlation. If it is significant at the .01 level or lower, ** will appear next to the correlation. For example, the correlation in the output at right has a **significance** level of < .001, so it is flagged with ** to indicate that it is less than .01.

To read the correlations, select a row and a column. For

Correlations

		height	weight	sex
height	Pearson Correlation	1	.806**	-.644**
	Sig. (2-tailed)		.000	.007
	N	16	16	16
weight	Pearson Correlation	.806**	1	-.968**
	Sig. (2-tailed)	.000		.000
	N	16	16	16
sex	Pearson Correlation	-.644**	-.968**	1
	Sig. (2-tailed)	.007	.000	
	N	16	16	16

**. Correlation is significant at the 0.01 level (2-tailed).

example, the correlation between height and weight is determined through selection of the WEIGHT row and the HEIGHT column (.806). We get the same answer by selecting the HEIGHT row and the WEIGHT column. The correlation between a variable and itself is always 1, so there is a diagonal set of 1s.

Drawing Conclusions

The correlation coefficient will be between –1.0 and +1.0. Coefficients close to 0.0 represent a weak relationship. Coefficients close to 1.0 or –1.0 represent a strong relationship. Generally, correlations greater than 0.7 are considered strong. Correlations less than 0.3 are considered weak. Correlations between 0.3 and 0.7 are considered moderate.

Significant correlations are flagged with asterisks. A significant correlation indicates a reliable relationship, but not necessarily a strong correlation. With enough participants, a very small correlation can be significant. Please see Appendix A for a discussion of **effect sizes** for correlations.

Phrasing a Significant Result

In the example above, we obtained a correlation of .806 between HEIGHT and WEIGHT. A correlation of .806 is a strong positive correlation, and it is significant at the .001 level. Thus, we could state the following in a results section:

A Pearson correlation coefficient was calculated for the relationship between participants' height and weight. A strong positive correlation was found ($r(14) = .806$, $p < .001$), indicating a significant linear relationship between the two variables. Taller participants tend to weigh more.

The conclusion states the direction (positive), strength (strong), value (.806), degrees of freedom (14), and **significance** level (< .001) of the correlation. In addition, a statement of direction is included (taller is heavier).

Note that the degrees of freedom given in parentheses is 14. The output indicates an N of 16. While most SPSS procedures give degrees of freedom, the correlation command gives only the N (the number of pairs). For a correlation, the degrees of freedom is $N - 2$.

Phrasing Results That Are Not Significant

Using our SAMPLE.sav data set from the previous chapters, we could calculate a correlation between ID and GRADE. If so, we get the output at right. The correlation has a **significance** level of .783. Thus, we could write the following in a results section (note that the degrees of freedom is $N - 2$):

Correlations

		ID	GRADE
ID	Pearson Correlation	1.000	.217
	Sig. (2-tailed)	.	.783
	N	4	4
GRADE	Pearson Correlation	.217	1.000
	Sig. (2-tailed)	.783	.
	N	4	4

A Pearson correlation was calculated examining the relationship between participants' ID numbers and grades. A weak correlation that was not significant was found ($r(2) = .217$, $p > .05$). ID number is not related to grade in the course.

Practice Exercise

Use Practice Data Set 2 in Appendix B. Determine the value of the Pearson correlation coefficient for the relationship between SALARY and YEARS OF EDUCATION.

Section 5.2 Spearman Correlation Coefficient

Description

The Spearman correlation coefficient determines the strength of the relationship between two variables. It is a nonparametric procedure. Therefore, it is weaker than the Pearson correlation coefficient, but it can be used in more situations.

Assumptions

Because the Spearman correlation coefficient functions on the basis of the ranks of data, it requires **ordinal** (or **interval** or **ratio**) data for both variables. They do not need to be normally distributed.

SPSS Data Format

Two variables are required in your SPSS data file. Each subject must provide data for both variables.

Running the Command

Click *Analyze*, then *Correlate*, then *Bivariate*. This will bring up the main **dialog box** for Bivariate Correlations (just like the Pearson correlation). About halfway down the **dialog box**, there is a section for indicating the type of correlation you will compute. You can select as many correlations as you want. For our example, remove the check in the *Pearson* box (by clicking on it) and click on the *Spearman* box.

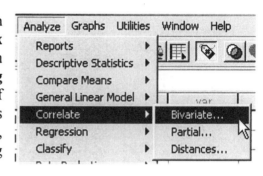

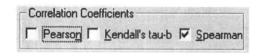

Use the variables HEIGHT and WEIGHT from our HEIGHT.sav data file (Chapter 4). This is also one of the few commands that allows you to choose a one-tailed test, if desired.

Reading the Output

The output is essentially the same as for the Pearson correlation. Each pair of variables has its correlation coefficient indicated twice. The Spearman *rho* can range from −1.0 to +1.0, just like the Pearson *r*.

Correlations

			HEIGHT	WEIGHT
Spearman's rho	HEIGHT	Correlation Coefficient	1.000	.883**
		Sig. (2-tailed)	.	.000
		N	16	16
	WEIGHT	Correlation Coefficient	.883**	1.000
		Sig. (2-tailed)	.000	.
		N	16	16

**. Correlation is significant at the .01 level (2-tailed).

The output listed above indicates a correlation of .883 between HEIGHT and WEIGHT. Note the **significance** level of .000, shown in the "Sig. (2-tailed)" row. This is, in fact, a **significance** level of < .001. The actual alpha level rounds out to .000, but it is not zero.

Drawing Conclusions

The correlation will be between −1.0 and +1.0. Scores close to 0.0 represent a weak relationship. Scores close to 1.0 or −1.0 represent a strong relationship. Significant correlations are flagged with asterisks. A significant correlation indicates a reliable relationship, but not necessarily a strong correlation. With enough participants, a very small correlation can be significant. Generally, correlations greater than 0.7 are considered strong. Correlations less than 0.3 are considered weak. Correlations between 0.3 and 0.7 are considered moderate.

Phrasing Results That Are Significant

In the example above, we obtained a correlation of .883 between HEIGHT and WEIGHT. A correlation of .883 is a strong positive correlation, and it is significant at the .001 level. Thus, we could state the following in a results section:

> A Spearman *rho* correlation coefficient was calculated for the relationship between participants' height and weight. A strong positive correlation was found (*rho* (14) = .883, *p* < .001), indicating a significant relationship between the two variables. Taller participants tend to weigh more.

The conclusion states the direction (positive), strength (strong), value (.883), degrees of freedom (14), and **significance** level (< .001) of the correlation. In addition, a statement of direction is included (taller is heavier). Note that the degrees of freedom given in parentheses is 14. The output indicates an *N* of 16. For a correlation, the degrees of freedom is $N - 2$.

Phrasing Results That Are Not Significant

Using our SAMPLE.sav data set from the previous chapters, we could calculate a Spearman *rho* correlation between ID and GRADE. If so, we would get the output at right. The correlation coefficient equals .000 and has a **significance** level of 1.000. Note that though this value is rounded up and is not, in fact, exactly 1.000, we could state the following in a results section:

Correlations

			ID	GRADE
Spearman's rho	ID	Correlation Coefficient	1.000	.000
		Sig. (2-tailed)	.	1.000
		N	4	4
	GRADE	Correlation Coefficient	.000	1.000
		Sig. (2-tailed)	1.000	.
		N	4	4

> A Spearman *rho* correlation coefficient was calculated for the relationship between a subject's ID number and grade. An extremely weak correlation that was not significant was found (*r* (2) = .000, *p* > .05). ID number is not related to grade in the course.

Practice Exercise

Use Practice Data Set 2 in Appendix B. Determine the strength of the relationship between salary and job classification by calculating the Spearman *rho* correlation.

Section 5.3 Simple Linear Regression

Description

Simple linear regression allows the prediction of one variable from another.

Assumptions

Simple linear regression assumes that both variables are **interval-** or **ratio-scaled**. In addition, the **dependent variable** should be normally distributed around the prediction line. This, of course, assumes that the variables are related to each other linearly. Typically, both variables should be normally distributed. **Dichotomous variables** (variables with only two **levels**) are also acceptable as **independent variables**.

SPSS Data Format

Two variables are required in the SPSS data file. Each subject must contribute to both values.

Running the Command

Click *Analyze*, then *Regression*, then *Linear*. This will bring up the main **dialog box** for Linear Regression. On the left side of the **dialog box** is a list of the variables in your data file (we are using the HEIGHT.sav data file from the start of this section). On the right are blocks for the **dependent variable** (the variable you are trying to predict), and the **independent variable** (the variable from which we are predicting).

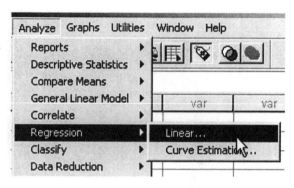

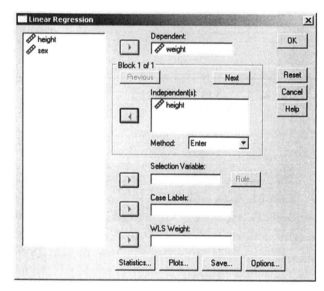

We are interested in predicting someone's weight on the basis of his or her height. Thus, we should place the variable WEIGHT in the **dependent variable** block and the variable HEIGHT in the **independent variable** block. Then we can click *OK* to run the analysis.

Reading the Output

For simple linear regressions, we are interested in three components of the output. The first is called the Model Summary, and it occurs after the Variables Entered/Removed section. For our example, you should see this output. *R* Square (called the **coefficient of determination**) gives you the proportion of the **variance** of your **dependent variable** (WEIGHT) that can be explained by variation in your **independent variable** (HEIGHT). Thus, 64.9% of the variation in weight can be explained by differences in height (taller individuals weigh more).

The **standard error of estimate** gives you a measure of dispersion for your prediction equation. When the prediction equation is used, 68% of the data will fall within

Model Summary

Model	R	R Square	Adjusted R Square	Std. Error of the Estimate
1	.806[a]	.649	.624	16.14801

a. Predictors: (Constant), height

one **standard error of estimate** (predicted) value. Just over 95% will fall within two standard errors. Thus, in the previous example, 95% of the time, our estimated weight will be within 32.296 pounds of being correct (i.e., 2 × 16.148 = 32.296).

ANOVA[b]

Model		Sum of Squares	df	Mean Square	F	Sig.
1	Regression	6760.323	1	6760.323	25.926	.000[a]
	Residual	3650.614	14	260.758		
	Total	10410.938	15			

a. Predictors: (Constant), HEIGHT

b. Dependent Variable: WEIGHT

The second part of the output that we are interested in is the ANOVA summary table, as shown above. The important number here is the **significance** level in the rightmost column. If that value is less than .05, then we have a significant linear regression. If it is larger than .05, we do not.

The final section of the output is the table of coefficients. This is where the actual prediction equation can be found.

Coefficients[a]

Model		Unstandardized Coefficients		Standardized Coefficients	t	Sig.
		B	Std. Error	Beta		
1	(Constant)	-234.681	71.552		-3.280	.005
	height	5.434	1.067	.806	5.092	.000

a. Dependent Variable: weight

In most texts, you learn that $Y' = a + bX$ is the regression equation. Y' (pronounced "Y prime") is your **dependent variable** (primes are normally predicted values or dependent variables), and X is your **independent variable**. In SPSS output, the values of both a and b are found in the B column. The first value, −234.681, is the value of a (labeled Constant). The second value, 5.434, is the value of b (labeled with the name of the **independent variable**). Thus, our prediction equation for the example above is WEIGHT' = −234.681 + 5.434 (HEIGHT). In other words, the average subject who is an inch taller than another subject weighs 5.434 pounds more. A person who is 60 inches tall should weigh −234.681 + 5.434(60) = 91.359 pounds. Given our earlier discussion of **standard error of estimate**, 95% of individuals who are 60 inches tall will weigh between 59.063 (91.359 − 32.296 = 59.063) and 123.655 (91.359 + 32.296 = 123.655) pounds.

Drawing Conclusions

Conclusions from regression analyses indicate (a) whether or not a significant prediction equation was obtained, (b) the direction of the relationship, and (c) the equation itself.

Phrasing Results That Are Significant

In the examples on pages 46 and 47, we obtained an *R* Square of .649 and a regression equation of WEIGHT' = –234.681 + 5.434 (HEIGHT). The ANOVA resulted in *F* = 25.926 with 1 and 14 degrees of freedom. The *F* is significant at the less than .001 level. Thus, we could state the following in a results section:

> A simple linear regression was calculated predicting participants' weight based on their height. A significant regression equation was found ($F(1,14) = 25.926$, $p < .001$), with an R^2 of .649. Participants' predicted weight is equal to –234.68 + 5.43 (HEIGHT) pounds when height is measured in inches. Participants' average weight increased 5.43 pounds for each inch of height.

The conclusion states the direction (increase), strength (.649), value (25.926), degrees of freedom (1,14), and **significance** level (< .001) of the regression. In addition, a statement of the equation itself is included.

Phrasing Results That Are Not Significant

If the ANOVA is not significant (e.g., see the output at right), the section of the output labeled *Sig.* for the ANOVA will be greater than .05, and the regression equation is not significant. A results section might include the following statement:

> A simple linear regression was calculated predicting participants' *ACT* scores based on their height. The regression equation was not significant ($F(1,14) = 4.12$, $p > .05$) with an R^2 of .227. Height is not a significant predictor of *ACT* scores.

Model Summary

Model	R	R Square	Adjusted R Square	Std. Error of the Estimate
1	.477ᵃ	.227	.172	3.06696

a. Predictors: (Constant), height

ANOVAᵇ

Model		Sum of Squares	df	Mean Square	F	Sig.
1	Regression	38.750	1	38.750	4.120	.062ᵃ
	Residual	131.688	14	9.406		
	Total	170.438	15			

a. Predictors: (Constant), height
b. Dependent Variable: act

Coefficientsᵃ

Model		Unstandardized Coefficients		Standardized Coefficients		
		B	Std. Error	Beta	t	Sig.
1	(Constant)	49.351	13.590		3.632	.003
	height	–.411	.203	–.477	–2.030	.062

a. Dependent Variable: act

Note that for results that are not significant, the ANOVA results and R^2 results are given, but the regression equation is not.

Practice Exercise

Use Practice Data Set 2 in Appendix B. If we want to predict salary from years of education, what salary would you predict for someone with 12 years of education? What salary would you predict for someone with a college education (16 years)?

Section 5.4   Multiple Linear Regression

Description

The multiple linear regression analysis allows the prediction of one variable from several other variables.

Assumptions

Multiple linear regression assumes that all variables are **interval-** or **ratio-scaled**. In addition, the **dependent variable** should be normally distributed around the prediction line. This, of course, assumes that the variables are related to each other linearly. All variables should be normally distributed. **Dichotomous variables** are also acceptable as **independent variables**.

SPSS Data Format

At least three variables are required in the SPSS data file. Each subject must contribute to all values.

Running the Command

Click *Analyze*, then *Regression*, then *Linear*. This will bring up the main **dialog box** for Linear Regression. On the left side of the **dialog box** is a list of the variables in your data file (we are using the HEIGHT.sav data file from the start of this chapter). On the right side of the **dialog box** are blanks for the **dependent variable** (the variable you are trying to predict) and the **independent variables** (the variables from which you are predicting).

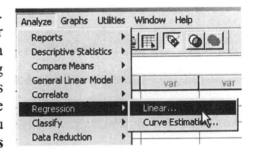

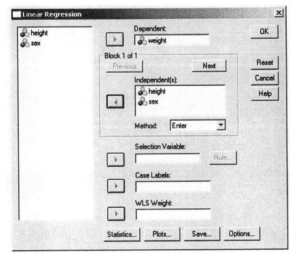

We are interested in predicting someone's weight based on his or her height and sex. We believe that both sex and height influence weight. Thus, we should place the **dependent variable** WEIGHT in the *Dependent* block and the **independent variables** HEIGHT and SEX in the *Independent(s)* block. Enter both in Block 1.

This will perform an analysis to determine if WEIGHT can be predicted from SEX and/or HEIGHT. There are several methods SPSS can use to conduct this analysis. These can be selected with the *Method* box. Method *Enter*, the most widely used, puts all variables in the equation, whether they are significant or not. The other methods use various means to enter only those variables that are significant predictors. Click *OK* to run the analysis.

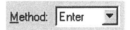

Reading the Output

For multiple linear regression, there are three components of the output in which we are interested. The first is called the Model Summary, which is found after the

Model Summary

Model	R	R Square	Adjusted R Square	Std. Error of the Estimate
1	.997[a]	.993	.992	2.29571

a. Predictors: (Constant), sex, height

Variables Entered/Removed section. For our example, you should get the output above. *R* Square (called the **coefficient of determination**) tells you the proportion of the **variance** in the **dependent variable** (WEIGHT) that can be explained by variation in the **independent variables** (HEIGHT and SEX, in this case). Thus, 99.3% of the variation in weight can be explained by differences in height and sex (taller individuals weigh more, and men weigh more). Note that when a second variable is added, our *R* Square goes up from .649 to .993. The .649 was obtained using the Simple Linear Regression example in Section 5.3.

The Standard Error of the Estimate gives you a margin of error for the prediction equation. Using the prediction equation, 68% of the data will fall within one **standard error of estimate** (predicted) value. Just over 95% will fall within two **standard errors of estimates**. Thus, in the example above, 95% of the time, our estimated weight will be within 4.591 (2.296 × 2) pounds of being correct. In our Simple Linear Regression example in Section 5.3, this number was 32.296. Note the higher degree of accuracy.

The second part of the output that we are interested in is the ANOVA summary table. For more information on reading ANOVA tables, refer to the sections on ANOVA in Chapter 6. For now, the important number is the **significance** in the rightmost column. If that value is less than .05, we have a significant linear regression. If it is larger than .05, we do not.

ANOVA[b]

Model		Sum of Squares	df	Mean Square	F	Sig.
1	Regression	10342.424	2	5171.212	981.202	.000[a]
	Residual	68.514	13	5.270		
	Total	10410.938	15			

a. Predictors: (Constant), sex, height

b. Dependent Variable: weight

The final section of output we are interested in is the table of coefficients. This is where the actual prediction equation can be found.

Coefficients[a]

Model		Unstandardized Coefficients		Standardized Coefficients		
		B	Std. Error	Beta	t	Sig.
1	(Constant)	47.138	14.843		3.176	.007
	height	2.101	.198	.312	10.588	.000
	sex	-39.133	1.501	-.767	-26.071	.000

a. Dependent Variable: weight

In most texts, you learn that $Y' = a + bX$ is the regression equation. For multiple regression, our equation changes to $Y' = B_0 + B_1X_1 + B_2X_2 + \ldots + B_zX_z$ (where z is the number of Independent Variables). Y' is your **dependent variable**, and the Xs are your **independent variables**. The Bs are listed in a column. Thus, our prediction equation for the example above is WEIGHT' = 47.138 – 39.133(SEX) + 2.101(HEIGHT) (where SEX is coded as 1 = Male, 2 = Female, and HEIGHT is in inches). In other words, the average difference in weight for participants who differ by one inch in height is 2.101 pounds. Males tend to weigh 39.133 pounds more than females. A female who is 60 inches tall should weigh 47.138 – 39.133(2) + 2.101(60) = 94.932 pounds. Given our earlier discussion of the **standard error of estimate**, 95% of females who are 60 inches tall will weigh between 90.341 (94.932 – 4.591 = 90.341) and 99.523 (94.932 + 4.591 = 99.523) pounds.

Drawing Conclusions

Conclusions from regression analyses indicate (a) whether or not a significant prediction equation was obtained, (b) the direction of the relationship, and (c) the equation itself. Multiple regression is generally much more powerful than simple linear regression. Compare our two examples.

With multiple regression, you must also consider the **significance** level of each **independent variable**. In the example above, the **significance** level of both **independent variables** is less than .001.

Phrasing Results That Are Significant

In our example, we obtained an R Square of .993 and a regression equation of WEIGHT' = 47.138 – 39.133(SEX) + 2.101(HEIGHT). The ANOVA resulted in $F = 981.202$ with 2 and 13 degrees of freedom. F is significant at the less than .001 level. Thus, we could state the following in a results section:

Model Summary

Model	R	R Square	Adjusted R Square	Std. Error of the Estimate
1	.997[a]	.993	.992	2.29571

a. Predictors: (Constant), sex, height

ANOVA[b]

Model		Sum of Squares	df	Mean Square	F	Sig.
1	Regression	10342.424	2	5171.212	981.202	.000[a]
	Residual	68.514	13	5.270		
	Total	10410.938	15			

a. Predictors: (Constant), sex, height

b. Dependent Variable: weight

Coefficients[a]

Model		Unstandardized Coefficients		Standardized Coefficients		
		B	Std. Error	Beta	t	Sig.
1	(Constant)	47.138	14.843		3.176	.007
	height	2.101	.198	.312	10.588	.000
	sex	-39.133	1.501	-.767	-26.071	.000

a. Dependent Variable: weight

A multiple linear regression was calculated to predict participants' weight based on their height and sex. A significant regression equation was found ($F_{(2,13)}$ = 981.202, p < .001), with an R^2 of .993. Participants' predicted weight is equal to 47.138 − 39.133(SEX) + 2.101(HEIGHT), where SEX is coded as 1 = Male, 2 = Female, and HEIGHT is measured in inches. Participants increased 2.101 pounds for each inch of height, and males weighed 39.133 pounds more than females. Both sex and height were significant predictors.

The conclusion states the direction (increase), strength (.993), value (981.20), degrees of freedom (2,13), and **significance** level (< .001) of the regression. In addition, a statement of the equation itself is included. Because there are multiple **independent variables**, we have noted whether or not each is significant.

Phrasing Results That Are Not Significant

If the ANOVA does not find a significant relationship, the *Sig.* section of the output will be greater than .05, and the regression equation is not significant. A results section for the output at right might include the following statement:

A multiple linear regression was calculated predicting participants' *ACT* scores based on their height and sex. The regression equation was not significant ($F_{(2,13)}$ = 2.511, p > .05) with an R^2 of .279. Neither height nor weight is a significant predictor of *ACT* scores.

Model Summary

Model	R	R Square	Adjusted R Square	Std. Error of the Estimate
1	.528a	.279	.168	3.07525

a. Predictors: (Constant), sex, height

ANOVAb

Model		Sum of Squares	df	Mean Square	F	Sig.
1	Regression	47.494	2	23.747	2.511	.120a
	Residual	122.944	13	9.457		
	Total	170.438	15			

a. Predictors: (Constant), sex, height
b. Dependent Variable: act

Coefficientsa

Model		Unstandardized Coefficients		Standardized Coefficients	t	Sig.
		B	Std. Error	Beta		
1	(Constant)	63.275	19.884		3.182	.007
	height	-.576	.266	-.668	-2.168	.049
	sex	-1.933	2.011	-.296	-.962	.354

a. Dependent Variable: act

Note that for results that are not significant, the ANOVA results and R^2 results are given, but the regression equation is not.

Practice Exercise

Use Practice Data Set 2 in Appendix B. Determine the prediction equation for predicting salary based on education, years of service, and sex. Which variables are significant predictors? If you believe that men were paid more than women were, what would you conclude after conducting this analysis?

Chapter 6

[handwritten note: t-test = assesses whether 2 groups are statistically different.]

Parametric Inferential Statistics

Parametric statistical procedures allow you to draw inferences about populations based on samples of those populations. To make these inferences, you must be able to make certain assumptions about the shape of the distributions of the population samples.

Section 6.1 Review of Basic Hypothesis Testing

The Null Hypothesis

In hypothesis testing, we create two hypotheses that are **mutually exclusive** (i.e., both cannot be true at the same time) and **all inclusive** (i.e., one of them must be true). We refer to those two hypotheses as the **null hypothesis** and the **alternative hypothesis**. The **null hypothesis** generally states that any difference we observe is caused by random error. The **alternative hypothesis** generally states that any difference we observe is caused by a systematic difference between groups.

Type I and Type II Errors

All hypothesis testing attempts to draw conclusions about the real world based on the results of a test (a statistical test, in this case). There are four possible combinations of results (see the figure at right).

Two of the possible results are correct test results. The other two results are errors. A **Type I error** occurs when we reject a **null hypothesis** that is, in fact, true, while a **Type II error** occurs when we fail to reject the **null hypothesis** that is, in fact, false.

Significance tests determine the probability of making a **Type I error**. In

REAL WORLD

	Null Hypothesis True	Null Hypothesis False
Reject Null Hypothesis	Type I Error	No Error
Fail to Reject Null Hypothesis	No Error	Type II Error

(Vertical axis label: TEST RESULTS)

other words, after performing a series of calculations, we obtain a probability that the **null hypothesis** is true. If there is a low probability, such as 5 or less in 100 (.05), by convention, we reject the **null hypothesis**. In other words, we typically use the .05 level (or less) as the maximum **Type I error** rate we are willing to accept.

When there is a low probability of a **Type I error**, such as .05, we can state that the **significance** test has led us to "reject the **null hypothesis**." This is synonymous with saying that a difference is "statistically significant." For example, on a reading test, suppose you found that a random sample of girls from a school district scored higher than a random sample of boys. This result may have been obtained merely because the chance errors associated with random sampling created the observed difference (this is what the **null hypothesis** asserts). If there is a sufficiently low probability that random errors were the cause (as determined by a **significance** test), we can state that the difference between boys and girls is statistically significant.

Significance Levels vs. Critical Values

Most statistics textbooks present hypothesis testing by using the concept of a critical value. With such an approach, we obtain a value for a test statistic and compare it to a critical value we look up in a table. If the obtained value is larger than the critical value, we reject the **null hypothesis** and conclude that we have found a significant difference (or relationship). If the obtained value is less than the critical value, we fail to reject the **null hypothesis** and conclude that there is not a significant difference.

The critical-value approach is well suited to hand calculations. Tables that give critical values for alpha levels of .001, .01, .05, etc., can be created. It is not practical to create a table for every possible alpha level.

On the other hand, SPSS can determine the exact alpha level associated with any value of a test statistic. Thus, looking up a critical value in a table is not necessary. This, however, does change the basic procedure for determining whether or not to reject the **null hypothesis**.

The section of SPSS output labeled *Sig.* (sometimes *p* or *alpha*) indicates the likelihood of making a **Type I error** if we reject the **null hypothesis**. A value of .05 or less indicates that we should reject the **null hypothesis** (assuming an alpha level of .05). A value greater than .05 indicates that we should fail to reject the **null hypothesis**.

In other words, when using SPSS, we normally reject the **null hypothesis** if the output value under *Sig.* is equal to or smaller than .05, and we fail to reject the **null hypothesis** if the output value is larger than .05.

One-Tailed vs. Two-Tailed Tests

SPSS output generally includes a two-tailed alpha level (normally labeled *Sig.* in the output). A two-tailed hypothesis attempts to determine whether any difference (either positive or negative) exists. Thus, you have an opportunity to make a **Type I error** on either of the two tails of the **normal distribution**.

A one-tailed test examines a difference in a specific direction. Thus, we can make a **Type I error** on only one side (tail) of the distribution. If we have a one-tailed hypothesis, but our SPSS output gives a two-tailed **significance** result, we can take the **significance** level in the output and divide it by two. Thus, if our difference is in the right direction, and if our output indicates a **significance** level of .084 (two-tailed), but we have a one-tailed hypothesis, we can report a **significance** level of .042 (one-tailed).

Phrasing Results

Results of hypothesis testing can be stated in different ways, depending on the conventions specified by your institution. The following examples illustrate some of these differences.

Degrees of Freedom

Sometimes the degrees of freedom are given in parentheses immediately after the symbol representing the test, as in this example:

$t(3) = 7.00, p < .01$

Other times, the degrees of freedom are given within the statement of results, as in this example:

$t = 7.00, df = 3, p < .01$

Significance Level

When you obtain results that are significant, they can be described in different ways. For example, if you obtained a **significance** level of .006 on a t test, you could describe it in any of the following three ways:

$t(3) = 7.00, p < .05$
$t(3) = 7.00, p < .01$
$t(3) = 7.00, p = .006$

Notice that because the exact probability is .006, both .05 and .01 are also correct.

There are also various ways of describing results that are not significant. For example, if you obtained a **significance** level of .505, any of the following three statements could be used:

$t(2) = .805, ns$
$t(2) = .805, p > .05$
$t(2) = .805, p = .505$

Statement of Results

Sometimes the results will be stated in terms of the **null hypothesis**, as in the following example:

The null hypothesis was rejected ($t = 7.00, df = 3, p = .006$).

Other times, the results are stated in terms of their level of **significance**, as in the following example:

A statistically significant difference was found: $t(3) = 7.00, p < .01$.

Statistical Symbols

Generally, statistical symbols are presented in *italics*. Prior to the widespread use of computers and desktop publishing, statistical symbols were underlined. Underlining is a signal to a printer that the underlined text should be set in italics. Institutions vary on their requirements for student work, so you are advised to consult your instructor about this.

Section 6.2   Single-Sample t Test

Description

The single-sample t test compares the **mean** of a single sample to a known population mean. It is useful for determining if the current set of data has changed from a long-term value (e.g., comparing the current year's temperatures to a historical average to determine if global warming is occurring).

Assumptions

The distributions from which the scores are taken should be normally distributed. However, the *t* test is **robust** and can handle violations of the assumption of a **normal distribution**. The **dependent variable** must be measured on an **interval** or **ratio scale**.

SPSS Data Format

The SPSS data file for the single-sample *t* test requires a single variable in SPSS. That variable represents the set of scores in the sample that we will compare to the population mean.

Running the Command

The single-sample *t* test is located in the *Compare Means* submenu, under the *Analyze* menu. The **dialog box** for the single-sample *t* test requires that we transfer the variable

representing the current set of scores to the *Test Variable(s)* section. We must also enter the population average in the *Test Value* blank. The example presented here is testing the variable LENGTH against a population mean of 35 (this example uses a hypothetical data set).

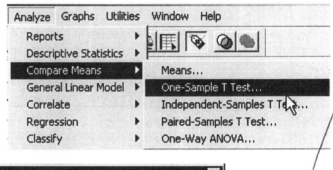

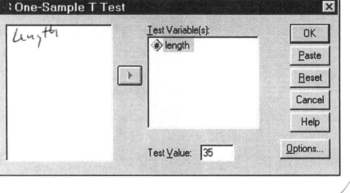

Reading the Output

The output for the single-sample *t* test consists of two sections. The first section lists the sample variable and some basic **descriptive statistics** (*N*, **mean**, **standard deviation**, and standard error).

T-Test

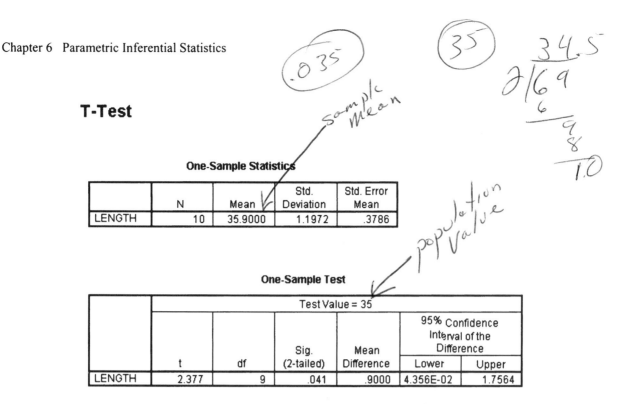

One-Sample Statistics

	N	Mean	Std. Deviation	Std. Error Mean
LENGTH	10	35.9000	1.1972	.3786

One-Sample Test

	Test Value = 35					
					95% Confidence Interval of the Difference	
	t	df	Sig. (2-tailed)	Mean Difference	Lower	Upper
LENGTH	2.377	9	.041	.9000	4.356E-02	1.7564

The second section of output contains the results of the *t* test. The example presented here indicates a *t* value of 2.377, with 9 degrees of freedom and a **significance** level of .041. The mean difference of .9000 is the difference between the sample average (35.90) and the population average we entered in the **dialog box** to conduct the test (35.00).

Drawing Conclusions

The *t* test assumes an equality of means. Therefore, a significant result indicates that the sample mean is not equivalent to the population mean (hence the term "significantly different"). A result that is not significant means that there is not a significant difference between the means. It does not mean that they are equal. Refer to your statistics text for the section on failure to reject the **null hypothesis**.

Phrasing Results That Are Significant

The above example found a significant difference between the population mean and the sample mean. Thus, we could state the following:

A single-sample *t* test compared the mean length of the sample to a population value of 35.00. A significant difference was found ($t(9)$ = 2.377, $p < .05$). The sample mean of 35.90 (*sd* = 1.197) was significantly greater than the population mean.

Phrasing Results That Are Not Significant

If the **significance** level had been greater than .05, the difference would not be significant. For example, if we received the output presented here, we could state the following:

One-Sample Statistics

	N	Mean	Std. Deviation	Std. Error Mean
temperature	9	68.6667	9.11043	3.03681

A single-sample *t* test compared the mean temperature over the past year to the long-term average.

One-Sample Test

	Test Value = 67.4					
					95% Confidence Interval of the Difference	
	t	df	Sig. (2-tailed)	Mean Difference	Lower	Upper
temperature	.417	8	.688	1.26667	-5.7362	8.2696

The difference was not significant ($t(8) = .417$, $p > .05$). The mean temperature over the past year was 68.67 ($sd = 9.11$) compared to the long-term average of 67.4.

Practice Exercise

The average salary in the U.S. is $25,000. Determine if the average salary of the participants in Practice Data Set 2 (Appendix B) is significantly greater than this value. Note that this is a one-tailed hypothesis.

Section 6.3 Independent-Samples *t* Test

Description

The independent-samples *t* test compares the means of two samples. The two samples are normally from randomly assigned groups.

Assumptions

The two groups being compared should be independent of each other. Observations are independent when information about one is unrelated to the other. Normally, this means that one group of participants provides data for one sample and a different group of participants provides data for the other sample (and individuals in one group are not matched with individuals in the other group). One way to accomplish this is through **random assignment** to form two groups.

The scores should be normally distributed, but the *t* test is **robust** and can handle violations of the assumption of a **normal distribution**.

The **dependent variable** must be measured on an **interval** or **ratio scale**. The **independent variable** should have only two **discrete** levels.

SPSS Data Format

The SPSS data file for the independent *t* test requires two variables. One variable, the **grouping variable**, represents the value of the **independent variable**. The **grouping variable** should have two distinct values (e.g., 0 for a control group and 1 for an experimental group). The second variable represents the **dependent variable**, such as scores on a test.

Conducting an Independent-Samples t Test

For our example, we will use the SAMPLE.sav data file.

Click *Analyze*, then *Compare Means*, then *Independent-Samples T Test*. This will bring up the main **dialog box**. Transfer the **dependent variable(s)** into the *Test Variable(s)* blank. For our example, we will use the variable GRADE.

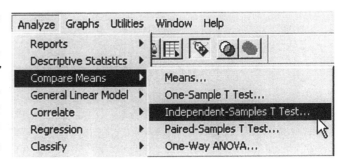

Transfer the **independent variable** into the *Grouping Variable* section. For our example, we will use the variable MORNING.

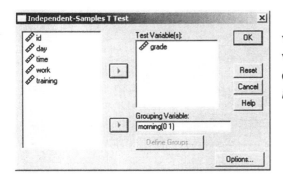

Next, click *Define Groups* and enter the values of the two **levels** of the **independent variable**. Independent *t* tests are capable of comparing only two **levels** at a time. Click *Continue*, then click *OK* to run the analysis.

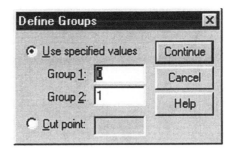

Output from the Independent-Samples t Test

The output will have a section labeled "Group Statistics." This section provides the basic **descriptive statistics** for the **dependent variable(s)** for each value of the **independent variable**. It should look like the output below.

Group Statistics

	morning	N	Mean	Std. Deviation	Std. Error Mean
grade	No	2	82.5000	3.53553	2.50000
	Yes	2	78.0000	7.07107	5.00000

Next, there will be a section with the results of the *t* test. It should look like the output below.

Independent Samples Test

		Levene's Test for Equality of Variances		t-test for Equality of Means						
		F	Sig.	t	df	Sig. (2-tailed)	Mean Difference	Std. Error Difference	95% Confidence Interval of the Difference	
									Lower	Upper
grade	Equal variances assumed	.	.	.805	2	.505	4.50000	5.59017	-19.55256	28.55256
	Equal variances not assumed			.805	1.471	.530	4.50000	5.59017	-30.09261	39.09261

The columns labeled *t*, *df*, and *Sig.* (*2-tailed*) provide the standard "answer" for the *t* test. They provide the value of *t*, the degrees of freedom (number of participants, minus 2, in this case), and the **significance** level (often called *p*). Normally, we use the "Equal variances assumed" row.

Drawing Conclusions

Recall from the previous section that the *t* test assumes an equality of **means**. Therefore, a significant result indicates that the **means** are not equivalent. When drawing conclusions about a *t* test, you must state the direction of the difference (i.e., which **mean** was larger than the other). You should also include information about the value of *t*, the degrees of freedom, the **significance** level, and the **means** and **standard deviations** for the two groups.

Phrasing Results That Are Significant

For a significant *t* test (for example, the output below), you might state the following:

Group Statistics

	group	N	Mean	Std. Deviation	Std. Error Mean
score	Control	4	41.0000	4.24264	2.12132
	Experimental	3	33.3333	2.08167	1.20185

Independent Samples Test

		Levene's Test for Equality of Variances		t-test for Equality of Means						
		F	Sig.	t	df	Sig. (2-tailed)	Mean Difference	Std. Error Difference	95% Confidence Interval of the Difference	
									Lower	Upper
score	Equal variances assumed	5.058	.074	2.835	5	.036	7.66667	2.70391	.71605	14.61728
	Equal variances not assumed			3.144	4.534	.029	7.66667	2.43812	1.20060	14.13273

An independent-samples *t* test comparing the mean scores of the experimental and control groups found a significant difference between the means of the two groups (*t*(5) = 2.835, *p* < .05). The mean of the experimental group was significantly lower (*m* = 33.333, *sd* = 2.08) than the mean of the control group (*m* = 41.000, *sd* = 4.24).

Phrasing Results That Are Not Significant

In our example at the start of the section, we compared the scores of the morning people to the scores of the nonmorning people. We did not find a significant difference, so we could state the following:

> An independent-samples *t* test was calculated comparing the mean score of participants who identified themselves as morning people to the mean score of participants who did not identify themselves as morning people. No significant difference was found ($t(2) = .805$, $p > .05$). The mean of the morning people ($m = 78.00$, $sd = 7.07$) was not significantly different from the mean of nonmorning people ($m = 82.50$, $sd = 3.54$).

Practice Exercise

Use Practice Data Set 1 (Appendix B) to solve this problem. We believe that young individuals have lower mathematics skills than older individuals. We would test this hypothesis by comparing participants 25 or younger (the "young" group) with participants 26 or older (the "old" group). Hint: You may need to create a new variable that represents which age group they are in. See Chapter 2 for help.

Section 6.4   Paired-Samples *t* Test

Description

The paired-samples *t* test (also called a dependent *t* test) compares the **means** of two scores from related samples. For example, comparing a pretest and a posttest score for a group of participants would require a paired-samples *t* test.

Assumptions

The paired-samples *t* test assumes that both variables are at the **interval** or **ratio** levels and are normally distributed. The two variables should also be measured with the same scale. If the scales are different, the scores should be converted to *z*-scores before the *t* test is conducted.

SPSS Data Format

Two variables in the SPSS data file are required. These variables should represent two measurements from each participant.

Running the Command ―*DO*

We will create a new data file containing five variables: PRETEST, MIDTERM, FINAL, INSTRUCT, and REQUIRED. INSTRUCT represents three different instructors for a course. REQUIRED represents whether the course was required or was an elective (0 = elective, 1 = required). The other three variables represent exam scores (100 being the highest score possible).

PRETEST	MIDTERM	FINAL	INSTRUCT	REQUIRED
56	64	69	1	0
79	91	89	1	0
68	77	81	1	0
59	69	71	1	1
64	77	75	1	1
74	88	86	1	1
73	85	86	1	1
47	64	69	2	0
78	98	100	2	0
61	77	85	2	0
68	86	93	2	1
64	77	87	2	1
53	67	76	2	1
71	85	95	2	1
61	79	97	3	0
57	77	89	3	0
49	65	83	3	0
71	93	100	3	1
61	83	94	3	1
58	75	92	3	1
58	74	92	3	1

Enter the data and save it as GRADES.sav. You can check your data entry by computing a **mean** for each instructor using the *Means* command (see Chapter 3 for more information). Use INSTRUCT as the **independent variable** and enter PRETEST, MIDTERM, and FINAL as your **dependent variables**.

Once you have entered the data, conduct a paired-samples *t* test comparing pretest scores and final scores.

Click *Analyze*, then *Compare Means*, then *Paired-Samples T Test*. This will bring up the main **dialog box**.

Report

INSTRUCT		PRETEST	MIDTERM	FINAL
1.00	Mean	67.5714	78.7143	79.5714
	N	7	7	7
	Std. Deviation	8.3837	9.9451	7.9552
2.00	Mean	63.1429	79.1429	86.4286
	N	7	7	7
	Std. Deviation	10.6055	11.7108	10.9218
3.00	Mean	59.2857	78.0000	92.4286
	N	7	7	7
	Std. Deviation	6.5502	8.6217	5.5032
Total	Mean	63.3333	78.6190	86.1429
	N	21	21	21
	Std. Deviation	8.9294	9.6617	9.6348

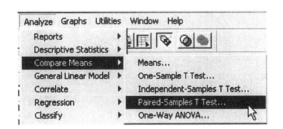

You must select pairs of variables to compare. As you select them, they are placed in the *Current Selections* area.

Click once on PRETEST, then once on FINAL. Both variables will be moved into the *Current Selections* area. Click on the right arrow to transfer the pair to the *Paired Variables* section. Click *OK* to conduct the test.

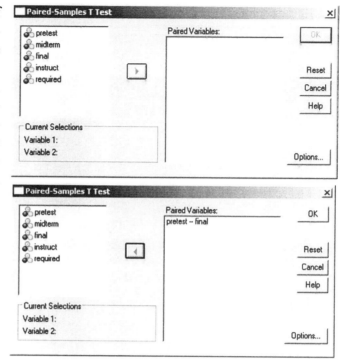

Reading the Output

The output for the paired-samples *t* test consists of three components. The first part gives you basic **descriptive statistics** for the

Paired Samples Statistics

		Mean	N	Std. Deviation	Std. Error Mean
Pair 1	PRETEST	63.3333	21	8.9294	1.9485
	FINAL	86.1429	21	9.6348	2.1025

pair of variables. The PRETEST average was 63.3, with a **standard deviation** of 8.93. The FINAL average was 86.14, with a **standard deviation** of 9.63.

Paired Samples Correlations

		N	Correlation	Sig.
Pair 1	PRETEST & FINAL	21	.535	.013

The second part of the output is a Pearson correlation coefficient for the pair of variables.

Within the third part of the output (on the next page), the section called *Paired Differences* contains information about the differences between the two variables. You may have learned in your statistics class that the paired-samples *t* test is essentially a single-sample *t* test calculated on the differences between the scores. The final three columns contain the value of *t*, the degrees of freedom, and the probability level. In the example presented here, we obtained a *t* of –11.646, with 20 degrees of freedom and a **significance** level of less than .001. Note that this is a two-tailed **significance** level. See the start of this chapter for more details on computing a one-tailed test.

Paired Samples Test

		Paired Differences						
					95% Confidence Interval of the Difference				
		Mean	Std. Deviation	Std. Error Mean	Lower	Upper	t	df	Sig. (2-tailed)
Pair 1	PRETEST - FINAL	-22.8095	8.9756	1.9586	-26.8952	-18.7239	-11.646	20	.000

Drawing Conclusions

Paired-samples *t* tests determine whether or not two scores are significantly different from each other. Significant values indicate that the two scores are different. Values that are not significant indicate that the scores are not significantly different.

Phrasing Results That Are Significant

When stating the results of a paired-samples *t* test, you should give the value of *t*, the degrees of freedom, and the **significance** level. You should also give the **mean** and **standard deviation** for each variable, as well as a statement of results that indicates whether you conducted a one- or two-tailed test. Our example above was significant, so we could state the following:

A paired-samples *t* test was calculated to compare the mean pretest score to the mean final exam score. The mean on the pretest was 63.33 (*sd* = 8.93), and the mean on the posttest was 86.14 (*sd* = 9.63). A significant increase from pretest to final was found (*t*(20) = –11.646, *p* < .001).

Phrasing Results That Are Not Significant

If the **significance** level had been greater than .05 (or greater than .10 if you were conducting a one-tailed test), the result would not have been significant. For example, the hypothetical output below represents a nonsignificant difference. For this output, we could state:

Paired Samples Statistics

		Mean	N	Std. Deviation	Std. Error Mean
Pair 1	midterm	78.7143	7	9.94509	3.75889
	final	79.5714	7	7.95523	3.00680

Paired Samples Correlations

		N	Correlation	Sig.
Pair 1	midterm & final	7	.969	.000

Paired Samples Test

		Paired Differences							
					95% Confidence Interval of the Difference				
		Mean	Std. Deviation	Std. Error Mean	Lower	Upper	t	df	Sig. (2-tailed)
Pair 1	midterm - final	-.85714	2.96808	1.12183	-3.60216	1.88788	-.764	6	.474

A paired-samples *t* test was calculated to compare the mean midterm score to the mean final exam score. The mean on the midterm was 78.71 (*sd* = 9.95), and the mean on the final was 79.57 (*sd* = 7.96). No significant difference from midterm to final was found (*t*(6) = −.764, *p* > .05).

Practice Exercise

Use the same GRADES.sav data file, and compute a paired-samples *t* test to determine if scores increased from midterm to final.

Section 6.5   One-Way ANOVA

Description

Analysis of variance (ANOVA) is a procedure that determines the proportion of variability attributed to each of several components. It is one of the most useful and adaptable statistical techniques available.

The one-way ANOVA compares the means of two or more groups of participants that vary on a single **independent variable** (thus, the one-way designation). When we have three groups, we could use a *t* test to determine differences between groups, but we would have to conduct three *t* tests (Group 1 compared to Group 2, Group 1 compared to Group 3, and Group 2 compared to Group 3). When we conduct multiple *t* tests, we inflate the **Type I error** rate and increase our chance of drawing an inappropriate conclusion. ANOVA compensates for these multiple comparisons and gives us a single answer that tells us if any of the groups is different from any of the other groups.

Assumptions

The one-way ANOVA requires a single **dependent variable** and a single **independent variable**. Which group participants belong to is determined by the value of the **independent variable**. Groups should be independent of each other. If our participants belong to more than one group each, we will have to conduct a repeated-measures ANOVA. If we have more than one **independent variable**, we would conduct a factorial ANOVA.

ANOVA also assumes that the **dependent variable** is at the **interval** or **ratio** levels and is normally distributed.

SPSS Data Format

Two variables are required in the SPSS data file. One variable serves as the **dependent variable** and the other as the **independent variable**. Each participant should provide only one score for the **dependent variable**.

Running the Command

For this example, we will use the GRADES.sav data file we created in the previous section.

To conduct a one-way ANOVA, click *Analyze*, then *Compare Means*, then *One-Way ANOVA*. This will bring up the main **dialog box** for the *One-Way ANOVA* command.

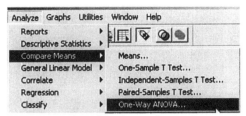

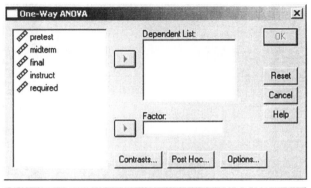

You should place the **independent variable** in the *Factor* box. For our example, INSTRUCT represents three different instructors, and it will be used as our **independent variable**.

Our **dependent variable** will be FINAL. This test will allow us to determine if the instructor has any effect on final grades in the course.

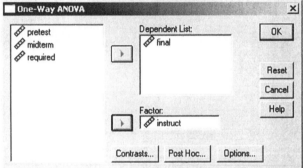

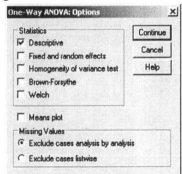

Click on the *Options* box to get the Options **dialog box**. Click *Descriptive*. This will give you means for the **dependent variable** at each **level** of the **independent variable**. Checking this box prevents us from having to run a separate means command. Click *Continue* to return to the main **dialog box**. Next, click *Post Hoc* to bring up the Post Hoc Multiple Comparisons **dialog box**. Click *Tukey*, then *Continue*.

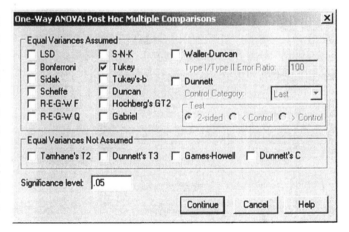

Post-hoc tests are necessary in the event of a significant ANOVA. The ANOVA only indicates if any group is different from any other group. If it is significant, we need to determine which groups are different from which other groups. We could do *t* tests to determine that, but we would have the same problem as before with inflating the **Type I error** rate.

There are a variety of post-hoc comparisons that correct for the multiple comparisons. The most widely used is **Tukey's *HSD***. SPSS will calculate a variety of post-hoc tests for you. Consult an advanced statistics text for a discussion of the differences between these various tests. Now click *OK* to run the analysis.

Reading the Output

Descriptive statistics will be given for each instructor (i.e., level of the **independent variable**) and the total. For example, in his/her class, Instructor 1 had an average final exam score of 79.57.

Descriptives

final

	N	Mean	Std. Deviation	Std. Error	95% Confidence Interval for Mean Lower Bound	Upper Bound	Minimum	Maximum
1.00	7	79.5714	7.95523	3.00680	72.2141	86.9288	69.00	89.00
2.00	7	86.4286	10.92180	4.12805	76.3276	96.5296	69.00	100.00
3.00	7	92.4286	5.50325	2.08003	87.3389	97.5182	83.00	100.00
Total	21	86.1429	9.63476	2.10248	81.7572	90.5285	69.00	100.00

ANOVA

final

	Sum of Squares	df	Mean Square	F	Sig.
Between Groups	579.429	2	289.714	4.083	.034
Within Groups	1277.143	18	70.952		
Total	1856.571	20			

The next section of the output is the ANOVA source table. This is where the various components of the **variance** have been listed, along with their relative sizes. For a one-way ANOVA, there are two components to the variance: Between Groups (which represents the differences due to our **independent variable**) and Within Groups (which represents differences within each level of our **independent variable**). For our example, the Between Groups variance represents differences due to different instructors. The Within Groups variance represents individual differences in students.

The primary answer is *F. F* is a ratio of explained **variance** to unexplained **variance**. Consult a statistics text for more information on how it is determined. The *F* has two different degrees of freedom, one for Between Groups (in this case, 2 is the number of **levels** of our **independent variable** [3 − 1]), and another for Within Groups (18 is the number of participants minus the number of **levels** of our **independent variable** [21 − 3]).

The next part of the output consists of the results of our **Tukey's *HSD*** post-hoc comparison.

This table presents us with every possible combination of levels of our **independent variable**. The first row represents Instructor 1 compared to Instructor 2. Next is Instructor 1 compared to Instructor 3. Next is Instructor 2 compared to Instructor 1. (Note that this is redundant with the first row.) Next is Instructor 2 compared to Instructor 3, and so on.

The column labeled *Sig.* represents the **Type I error** (*p*) rate for the simple (2-level) comparison in that row. In our

Multiple Comparisons

Dependent Variable: FINAL
Tukey HSD

(I) INSTRUCT	(J) INSTRUCT	Mean Difference (I-J)	Std. Error	Sig.	95% Confidence Interval Lower Bound	Upper Bound
1.00	2.00	-6.8571	4.502	.304	-18.3482	4.6339
	3.00	-12.8571*	4.502	.027	-24.3482	-1.3661
2.00	1.00	6.8571	4.502	.304	-4.6339	18.3482
	3.00	-6.0000	4.502	.396	-17.4911	5.4911
3.00	1.00	12.8571*	4.502	.027	1.3661	24.3482
	2.00	6.0000	4.502	.396	-5.4911	17.4911

*. The mean difference is significant at the .05 level.

example above, Instructor 1 is significantly different from Instructor 3, but Instructor 1 is not significantly different from Instructor 2, and Instructor 2 is not significantly different from Instructor 3.

Drawing Conclusions

Drawing conclusions for ANOVA requires that we indicate the value of F, the degrees of freedom, and the **significance** level. A significant ANOVA should be followed by the results of a post-hoc analysis and a verbal statement of the results.

Phrasing Results That Are Significant

In our example above, we could state the following:

We computed a one-way ANOVA comparing the final exam scores of participants who took a course from one of three different instructors. A significant difference was found among the instructors ($F(2,18) = 4.08$, $p < .05$). **Tukey's HSD** was used to determine the nature of the differences between the instructors. This analysis revealed that students who had Instructor 1 scored lower ($m = 79.57$, $sd = 7.96$) than students who had Instructor 3 ($m = 92.43$, $sd = 5.50$). Students who had Instructor 2 ($m = 86.43$, $sd = 10.92$) were not significantly different from either of the other two groups.

Phrasing Results That Are Not Significant

If we had conducted the analysis using PRETEST as our **dependent variable** instead of FINAL, we would have received the following output:

The ANOVA was not significant, so there is no need to refer to the Multiple Comparisons table. Given this result, we may state the following:

Descriptives

pretest

	N	Mean	Std. Deviation	Std. Error	95% Confidence Interval for Mean Lower Bound	Upper Bound	Minimum	Maximum
1.00	7	67.5714	8.38366	3.16872	59.8178	75.3250	56.00	79.00
2.00	7	63.1429	10.60548	4.00849	53.3344	72.9513	47.00	78.00
3.00	7	59.2857	6.55017	2.47573	53.2278	65.3436	49.00	71.00
Total	21	63.3333	8.92935	1.94854	59.2687	67.3979	47.00	79.00

ANOVA

pretest

	Sum of Squares	df	Mean Square	F	Sig.
Between Groups	240.667	2	120.333	1.600	.229
Within Groups	1354.000	18	75.222		
Total	1594.667	20			

The pretest means of students who took a course from three different instructors were compared using a one-way ANOVA. No significant difference was found ($F(2,18) = 1.60$, $p > .05$). The students from the three different classes did not differ significantly at the start of the term. Students who had Instructor 1 had a mean score of 67.57 ($sd = 8.38$). Students who had Instructor 2 had a mean score of 63.14 ($sd = 10.61$). Students who had Instructor 3 had a mean score of 59.29 ($sd = 6.55$).

Practice Exercise

Using Practice Data Set 1 in Appendix B, determine if the average math scores of single, married, and divorced participants are significantly different. Write a statement of results.

Section 6.6   Factorial ANOVA

Description

The factorial ANOVA is one in which there is more than one **independent variable**. A 2 × 2 ANOVA, for example, has two **independent variables**, each with two **levels**. A 3 × 2 × 2 ANOVA has three **independent variables**. One has three **levels**, and the other two have two **levels**. Factorial ANOVA is very powerful because it allows us to assess the effects of each **independent variable**, plus the effects of the **interaction**.

Assumptions

Factorial ANOVA requires all of the assumptions of one-way ANOVA (i.e., the **dependent variable** must be at the **interval** or **ratio** levels and normally distributed). In addition, the **independent variables** should be independent of each other.

SPSS Data Format

SPSS requires one variable for the **dependent variable**, and one variable for each **independent variable**. If we have *any* **independent variable** that is represented as multiple variables (e.g., PRETEST and POSTTEST), we must use the repeated-measures ANOVA.

Running the Command

This example uses the GRADES.sav data file from earlier in this chapter. Click *Analyze*, then *General Linear Model*, then *Univariate*.

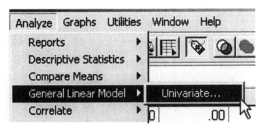

This will bring up the main **dialog box** for Univariate ANOVA. Select the **dependent variable** and place it in the *Dependent Variable* blank (use FINAL for this example). Select one of your **independent variables** (INSTRUCT, in this case) and place it in the *Fixed Factor(s)* box. Place the second **independent variable** (REQUIRED) in the *Fixed Factor(s)*

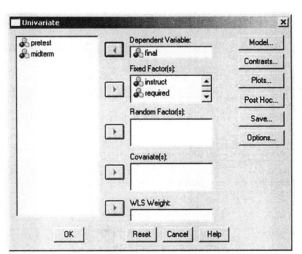

box. Having defined the analysis, now click *Options*.

When the Options **dialog box** comes up, move INSTRUCT, REQUIRED, and INSTRUCT × REQUIRED into the *Display Means for* blank. This will provide you with **means** for each main effect and **interaction** term. Click *Continue*.

If you were to select *Post-Hoc*, SPSS would run post-hoc analyses for the main effects but not for the **interaction** term. Click *OK* to run the analysis.

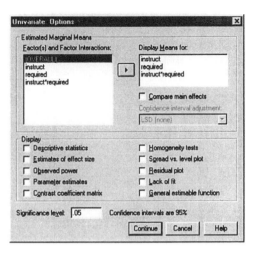

1. INSTRUCT

Dependent Variable: FINAL

INSTRUCT	Mean	Std. Error	95% Confidence Interval	
			Lower Bound	Upper Bound
1.00	79.583	3.445	72.240	86.926
2.00	86.208	3.445	78.865	93.551
3.00	92.083	3.445	84.740	99.426

2. REQUIRED

Dependent Variable: FINAL

REQUIRED	Mean	Std. Error	95% Confidence Interval	
			Lower Bound	Upper Bound
.00	84.667	3.007	78.257	91.076
1.00	87.250	2.604	81.699	92.801

Reading the Output

At the bottom of the output, you will find the means for each main effect and **interaction** you selected with the *Options* command.

There were three instructors, so there is a **mean** FINAL for each instructor. We also have **means** for the two values of REQUIRED. Finally, we have six **means** representing the **interaction** of the two variables (this was a 3 × 2 design).

Participants who had Instructor 1 (for whom the class was not required) had a **mean** final exam score of 79.67. Students who had Instructor 1 (for whom it was required) had a **mean** final exam score of 79.50, and so on.

The example we just ran is called a two-way ANOVA. This is because we had two **independent variables**. With a two-way ANOVA, we get three answers: a main effect for INSTRUCT, a main effect for REQUIRED, and an **interaction** result for INSTRUCT × REQUIRED (see top of next page).

3. INSTRUCT * REQUIRED

Dependent Variable: FINAL

INSTRUCT	REQUIRED	Mean	Std. Error	95% Confidence Interval	
				Lower Bound	Upper Bound
1.00	.00	79.667	5.208	68.565	90.768
	1.00	79.500	4.511	69.886	89.114
2.00	.00	84.667	5.208	73.565	95.768
	1.00	87.750	4.511	78.136	97.364
3.00	.00	89.667	5.208	78.565	100.768
	1.00	94.500	4.511	84.886	104.114

Tests of Between-Subjects Effects

Dependent Variable: FINAL

Source	Type III Sum of Squares	df	Mean Square	F	Sig.
Corrected Model	635.821[a]	5	127.164	1.563	.230
Intercept	151998.893	1	151998.893	1867.691	.000
INSTRUCT	536.357	2	268.179	3.295	.065
REQUIRED	34.321	1	34.321	.422	.526
INSTRUCT * REQUIRED	22.071	2	11.036	.136	.874
Error	1220.750	15	81.383		
Total	157689.000	21			
Corrected Total	1856.571	20			

a. R Squared = .342 (Adjusted R Squared = .123)

The source table above gives us these three answers (in the INSTRUCT, REQUIRED, and INSTRUCT * REQUIRED rows). In the example, none of the main effects or **interactions** was significant. In the statements of results, you must indicate F, two degrees of freedom (effect and residual/error), the **significance** level, and a verbal statement for each of the answers (three, in this case). Note that most statistics books give a much simpler version of an ANOVA source table where the Corrected Model, Intercept, and Corrected Total rows are not included.

Phrasing Results That Are Significant

If we had obtained significant results in this example, we could state the following (These are fictitious results. For the results that correspond to the example above, please see the section on phrasing results that are not significant):

A 3 (instructor) × 2 (required course) between-subjects factorial ANOVA was calculated comparing the final exam scores for participants who had one of three instructors and who took the course either as a required course or as an elective. A significant main effect for instructor was found ($F(2,15) = 10.112, p < .05$). Students who had Instructor 1 had higher final exam scores ($m = 79.57, sd = 7.96$) than students who had Instructor 3 ($m = 92.43, sd = 5.50$). Students who had Instructor 2 ($m = 86.43, sd = 10.92$) were not significantly different from either of the other two groups. A significant main effect for whether or not the course was required was found ($F(1,15) = 38.44, p < .01$). Students who took the course because it was required did better ($m = 91.69, sd = 7.68$) than students who took the course as an elective ($m = 77.13, sd = 5.72$). The interaction was not significant ($F(2,15) = 1.15, p > .05$). The effect of the instructor was not influenced by whether or not the students took the course because it was required.

Note that in the above example, we would have had to conduct **Tukey's *HSD*** to determine the differences for INSTRUCT (using the *Post-Hoc* command). This is not necessary for REQUIRED because it has only two **levels** (and one must be different from the other).

Phrasing Results That Are Not Significant

Our actual results were not significant, so we can state the following:

A 3 (instructor) × 2 (required course) between-subjects factorial ANOVA was calculated comparing the final exam scores for participants who had one of three instructors and who took the course as a required course or as an elective. The main effect for instructor was not significant ($F(2,15) = 3.30$, $p > .05$). The main effect for whether or not it was a required course was also not significant ($F(1,15) = .42$, $p > .05$). Finally, the interaction was also not significant ($F(2,15) = .136$, $p > .05$). Thus, it appears that neither the instructor nor whether or not the course is required has any significant effect on final exam scores.

Practice Exercise

Using Practice Data Set 2 in Appendix B, determine if salaries are influenced by sex, job classification, or an **interaction** between sex and job classification. Write a statement of results.

Section 6.7   Repeated-Measures ANOVA

Description

Repeated-measures ANOVA extends the basic ANOVA procedure to a within-subjects **independent variable** (when participants provide data for more than one **level** of an **independent variable**). It functions like a paired-samples *t* test when more than two **levels** are being compared.

Assumptions

The **dependent variable** should be normally distributed and measured on an **interval** or **ratio scale**. Multiple measurements of the **dependent variable** should be from the same (or related) participants.

SPSS Data Format

At least three variables are required. Each variable in the SPSS data file should represent a single **dependent variable** at a single **level** of the **independent variable**. Thus, an analysis of a design with four **levels** of an **independent variable** would require four variables in the SPSS data file.

If any variable represents a between-subjects effect, use the *Mixed-Design ANOVA* command instead.

Running the Command

This example uses the GRADES.sav sample data set. Recall that GRADES.sav includes three sets of grades—PRETEST, MIDTERM, and FINAL—that represent three different times during the semester. This allows us to analyze the effects of time on the test performance of our sample population (hence the within-groups comparison). Click *Analyze*, then *General Linear Model*, then *Repeated Measures*.

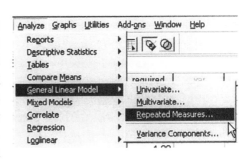

Note that this procedure requires an optional module. If you do not have this command, you do not have the proper module installed. This procedure is NOT included in the student version of SPSS.

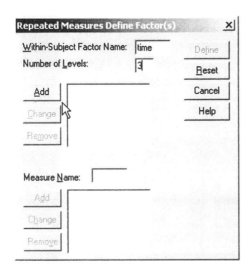

After selecting the command, you will be presented with the Repeated Measures Define Factor(s) **dialog box**. This is where you identify the within-subject factor (we will call it TIME). Enter 3 for the number of **levels** (three exams) and click *Add*.

Now click *Define*. If we had more than one **independent variable** that had repeated measures, we could enter its name and click *Add*.

You will be presented with the Repeated Measures **dialog box**. Transfer PRETEST, MIDTERM, and FINAL to the *Within-Subjects Variables* section. The variable names should be ordered according to when they occurred in time (i.e., the values of the **independent variable** that they represent).

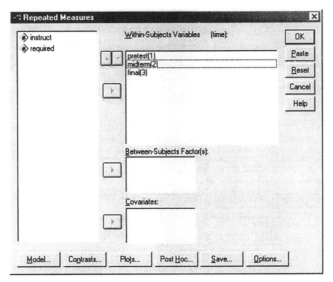

Click *Options*, and SPSS will compute the means for the TIME effect (see one-way ANOVA for more details about how to do this). Click *OK* to run the command.

Reading the Output

This procedure uses the *GLM* command. GLM stands for "General Linear Model." It is a very powerful command, and many sections of output are beyond the scope of this text (see output outline at right). But for the basic repeated-measures ANOVA, we are interested only in the *Tests of Within-Subjects Effects*. Note that the SPSS output will include many other sections of output, which you can ignore at this point.

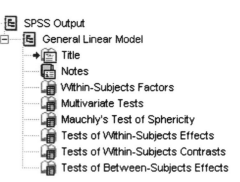

Tests of Within-Subjects Effects

Measure: MEASURE_1

Source		Type III Sum of Squares	df	Mean Square	F	Sig.
time	Sphericity Assumed	5673.746	2	2836.873	121.895	.000
	Greenhouse-Geisser	5673.746	1.211	4685.594	121.895	.000
	Huynh-Feldt	5673.746	1.247	4550.168	121.895	.000
	Lower-bound	5673.746	1.000	5673.746	121.895	.000
Error(time)	Sphericity Assumed	930.921	40	23.273		
	Greenhouse-Geisser	930.921	24.218	38.439		
	Huynh-Feldt	930.921	24.939	37.328		
	Lower-bound	930.921	20.000	46.546		

The *Tests of Within-Subjects Effects* output should look very similar to the output from the other *ANOVA* commands. In the above example, the effect of TIME has an *F* value of 121.90 with 2 and 40 degrees of freedom (we use the line for *Sphericity Assumed*). It is significant at less than the .001 level. When describing these results, we should indicate the type of test, *F* value, degrees of freedom, and **significance** level.

Phrasing Results That Are Significant

Because the ANOVA results were significant, we need to do some sort of post-hoc analysis. One of the main limitations of SPSS is the difficulty in performing post-hoc analyses for within-subjects factors. With SPSS, the easiest solution to this problem is to conduct **protected dependent *t* tests** with repeated-measures ANOVA. There are more powerful (and more appropriate) post-hoc analyses, but SPSS will not compute them for us. For more information, consult your instructor or a more advanced statistics text.

To conduct the protected *t* tests, we will compare PRETEST to MIDTERM, MIDTERM to FINAL, and PRETEST to FINAL, using paired-samples *t* tests. Because we are conducting three tests and, therefore, inflating our **Type I error** rate, we will use a **significance** level of .017 (.05/3) instead of .05.

Paired Samples Test

		Paired Differences							
					95% Confidence Interval of the Difference				
		Mean	Std. Deviation	Std. Error Mean	Lower	Upper	t	df	Sig. (2-tailed)
Pair 1	PRETEST - MIDTERM	-15.2857	3.9641	.8650	-17.0902	-13.4813	-17.670	20	.000
Pair 2	PRETEST - FINAL	-22.8095	8.9756	1.9586	-26.8952	-18.7239	-11.646	20	.000
Pair 3	MIDTERM - FINAL	-7.5238	6.5850	1.4370	-10.5213	-4.5264	-5.236	20	.000

The three comparisons each had a **significance** level of less than .017, so we can conclude that the scores improved from pretest to midterm and again from midterm to final. To generate the **descriptive statistics**, we have to run the *Descriptives* command for each variable.

Because the results of our example above were significant, we could state the following:

A one-way repeated-measures ANOVA was calculated comparing the exam scores of participants at three different times: pretest, midterm, and final. A significant effect was found ($F(2,40) = 121.90$, $p < .001$). Follow-up protected t tests revealed that scores increased significantly from pretest ($m = 63.33$, $sd = 8.93$) to midterm ($m = 78.62$, $sd = 9.66$), and again from midterm to final ($m = 86.14$, $sd = 9.63$).

Phrasing Results That Are Not Significant

With results that are not significant, we could state the following (the F values here have been made up for purposes of illustration):

A one-way repeated-measures ANOVA was calculated comparing the exam scores of participants at three different times: pretest, midterm, and final. No significant effect was found ($F(2,40) = 1.90$, $p > .05$). No significant difference exists among pretest ($m = 63.33$, $sd = 8.93$), midterm ($m = 78.62$, $sd = 9.66$), and final ($m = 86.14$, $sd = 9.63$) means.

Practice Exercise

Use Practice Data Set 3 in Appendix B. Determine if the anxiety level of participants changed over time (regardless of which treatment they received) using a one-way repeated-measures ANOVA and protected dependent t tests. Write a statement of results.

Section 6.8   Mixed-Design ANOVA

Description

The mixed-design ANOVA (sometimes called a split-plot design) tests the effects of more than one **independent variable**. At least one of the **independent variables** must be within-subjects (repeated measures). At least one of the **independent variables** must be between-subjects.

Assumptions

The **dependent variable** should be normally distributed and measured on an **interval** or **ratio scale**.

SPSS Data Format

The **dependent variable** should be represented as one variable for each level of the within-subjects **independent variables**. Another variable should be present in the data file for each between-subjects variable. Thus, a 2 × 2 mixed-design ANOVA would require three variables, two representing the **dependent variable** (one at each level), and one representing the between-subjects **independent variable**.

Running the Command

The *General Linear Model* command runs the *Mixed-Design ANOVA* command. Click *Analyze*, then *General Linear Model*, then *Repeated Measures*. **Note that this procedure requires an optional module. If you do not have this command, you do not have the proper module installed. This procedure is NOT included in the student version of SPSS.**

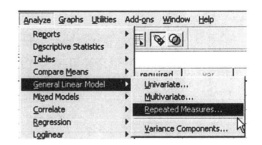

The *Repeated Measures* command should be used if any of the **independent variables** are repeated measures (within-subjects).

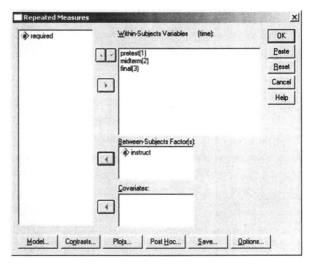

This example also uses the GRADES.sav data file. Enter PRETEST, MIDTERM, and FINAL in the *Within-Subjects Variables* block. (See the *Repeated Measures ANOVA* command in Section 6.7 for an explanation.) This example is a 3 × 3 mixed-design. There are two **independent variables** (TIME and INSTRUCT), each with three **levels**. We previously entered the information for TIME in the Repeated Measures Define Factors **dialog box**.

We need to transfer INSTRUCT into the *Between-Subjects Factor(s)* block.

Click *Options* and select means for all of the main effects and the **interaction** (see one-way ANOVA in Section 6.5 for more details about how to do this). Click *OK* to run the command.

Reading the Output

As with the standard repeated measures command, the GLM procedure provides a lot of output we will not use. For a mixed-design ANOVA, we are interested in two sections. The first is *Tests of Within-Subjects Effects*.

Tests of Within-Subjects Effects

Measure: MEASURE_1

Source		Type III Sum of Squares	df	Mean Square	F	Sig.
time	Sphericity Assumed	5673.746	2	2836.873	817.954	.000
	Greenhouse-Geisser	5673.746	1.181	4802.586	817.954	.000
	Huynh-Feldt	5673.746	1.356	4183.583	817.954	.000
	Lower-bound	5673.746	1.000	5673.746	817.954	.000
time * instruct	Sphericity Assumed	806.063	4	201.516	58.103	.000
	Greenhouse-Geisser	806.063	2.363	341.149	58.103	.000
	Huynh-Feldt	806.063	2.712	297.179	58.103	.000
	Lower-bound	806.063	2.000	403.032	58.103	.000
Error(time)	Sphericity Assumed	124.857	36	3.468		
	Greenhouse-Geisser	124.857	21.265	5.871		
	Huynh-Feldt	124.857	24.411	5.115		
	Lower-bound	124.857	18.000	6.937		

This section gives two of the three answers we need (the main effect for TIME and the interaction result for TIME × INSTRUCTOR). The second section of output is *Tests of Between-Subjects Effects* (sample output is below). Here, we get the answers that do not contain any within-subjects effects. For our example, we get the main effect for INSTRUCT. Both of these sections must be combined to produce the full answer for our analysis.

Tests of Between-Subjects Effects

Measure: MEASURE_1

Transformed Variable: Average

Source	Type III Sum of Squares	df	Mean Square	F	Sig.
Intercept	364192.063	1	364192.063	1500.595	.000
instruct	18.698	2	9.349	.039	.962
Error	4368.571	18	242.698		

If we obtain significant effects, we must perform some sort of post-hoc analysis. Again, this is one of the limitations of SPSS. No easy way to perform the appropriate post-hoc test for repeated-measures (within-subjects) factors is available. Ask your instructor for assistance with this.

When describing the results, you should include *F*, the degrees of freedom, and the **significance** level for each main effect and interaction. In addition, some **descriptive statistics** must be included (either give means or include a figure).

Phrasing Results That Are Significant

There are three answers (at least) for all mixed-design ANOVAs. Please see Section 6.6 on factorial ANOVA for more details about how to interpret and phrase the results.

For the above example, we could state the following in the results section (note that this assumes that appropriate post-hoc tests have been conducted):

A 3 × 3 mixed-design ANOVA was calculated to examine the effects of the instructor (Instructors 1, 2, and 3) and time (pretest, midterm, and final) on scores. A significant time × instructor interaction was present ($F(4,36) = 58.10$, $p < .001$). In addition, the main effect for time was significant ($F(2,36) = 817.95$, $p < .001$). The main effect for instructor was not significant ($F(2,18) = .039$, $p > .05$). Upon examination of the data, it appears that Instructor 3 showed the most improvement in scores over time.

With significant **interactions**, it is often helpful to provide a graph with the **descriptive statistics**. By selecting the *Plots* option in the main **dialog box**, you can make graphs of the **interaction** like the one below. **Interactions** add considerable complexity to the interpretation of statistical results. Consult a research methods text or ask your instructor for more help with **interactions**.

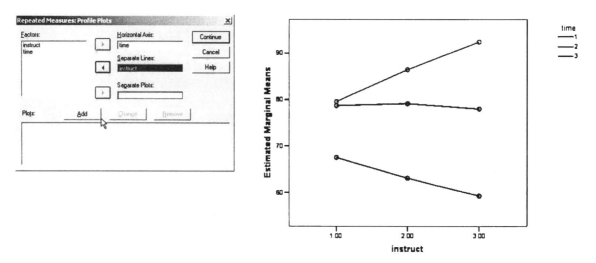

Phrasing Results That Are Not Significant

If our results had not been significant, we could state the following (note that the F values are fictitious):

A 3 × 3 mixed-design ANOVA was calculated to examine the effects of the instructor (Instructors 1, 2, and 3) and time (pretest, midterm, and final) on scores. No significant main effects or interactions were found. The time × instructor interaction ($F(4,36) = 1.10$, $p > .05$), the main effect for time ($F(2,36) = 1.95$, $p > .05$), and the main effect for instructor ($F(2,18) = .039$, $p > .05$) were all not significant. Exam scores were not influenced by either time or instructor.

Practice Exercise

Use Practice Data Set 3 in Appendix B. Determine if anxiety **levels** changed over time for each of the treatment (CONDITION) types. How did time change anxiety **levels** for each treatment? Write a statement of results.

Section 6.9 Analysis of Covariance

Description

Analysis of covariance (ANCOVA) allows you to remove the effect of a known **covariate**. In this way, it becomes a statistical method of control. With methodological controls (e.g., **random assignment**), internal **validity** is gained. When such methodological controls are not possible, statistical controls can be used.

ANCOVA can be performed by using the *GLM* command if you have repeated-measures factors. Because the *GLM* command is not included in the Base Statistics module, it is not included here.

Assumptions

ANCOVA requires that the **covariate** be significantly correlated with the **dependent variable**. The **dependent variable** and the **covariate** should be at the **interval** or **ratio levels**. In addition, both should be normally distributed.

SPSS Data Format

The SPSS data file must contain one variable for each **independent variable**, one variable representing the **dependent variable**, and at least one **covariate**.

Running the Command

The *Factorial ANOVA* command is used to run ANCOVA. To run it, click *Analyze*, then *General Linear Model*, then *Univariate*. Follow the directions discussed for factorial ANOVA, using the HEIGHT.sav sample data file. Place the variable HEIGHT as your *Dependent Variable*. Enter SEX as your *Fixed Factor*, then WEIGHT as the *Covariate*. This last step determines the difference between regular factorial ANOVA and ANCOVA. Click *OK* to run the ANCOVA.

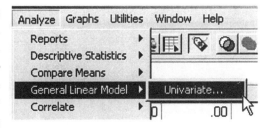

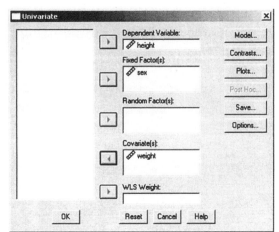

Reading the Output

The output consists of one main source table (shown below). This table gives you the main effects and **interactions** you would have received with a normal factorial ANOVA. In addition, there is a row for each **covariate**. In our example, we have one main effect (SEX) and one **covariate** (WEIGHT). Normally, we examine the **covariate** line only to confirm that the **covariate** is significantly related to the **dependent variable**.

Drawing Conclusions

This sample analysis was performed to determine if males and females differ in height, after weight is accounted for. We know that weight is related to height. Rather than match participants or use methodological controls, we can statistically remove the effect of weight.

When giving the results of ANCOVA, we must give *F*, degrees of freedom, and **significance** levels for all main effects, **interactions**, and **covariates**. If main effects or **interactions** are significant, post-hoc tests must be conducted. **Descriptive statistics (mean** and **standard deviation)** for each **level** of the **independent variable** should also be given.

Tests of Between-Subjects Effects

Dependent Variable: HEIGHT

Source	Type III Sum of Squares	df	Mean Square	F	Sig.
Corrected Model	215.027a	2	107.513	100.476	.000
Intercept	5.580	1	5.580	5.215	.040
WEIGHT	119.964	1	119.964	112.112	.000
SEX	66.367	1	66.367	62.023	.000
Error	13.911	13	1.070		
Total	71919.000	16			
Corrected Total	228.938	15			

a. R Squared = .939 (Adjusted R Squared = .930)

Phrasing Results That Are Significant

The above example obtained a significant result, so we could state the following:

A one-way between-subjects ANCOVA was calculated to examine the effect of sex on height, covarying out the effect of weight. Weight was significantly related to height ($F(1,13) = 112.11$, $p < .001$). The main effect for sex was significant ($F(1,13) = 62.02$, $p < .001$), with males significantly taller ($m = 69.38$, $sd = 3.70$) than females ($m = 64.50$, $sd = 2.33$).

Phrasing Results That Are Not Significant

If the **covariate** is not significant, we need to repeat the analysis without including the **covariate** (i.e., run a normal ANOVA).

For ANCOVA results that are not significant, you could state the following (note that the *F* values are made up for this example):

A one-way between-subjects ANCOVA was calculated to examine the effect of sex on height, covarying out the effect of weight. Weight was significantly related to height ($F(1,13) = 112.11, p < .001$). The main effect for sex was not significant ($F(1,13) = 2.02, p > .05$), with males not being significantly taller ($m = 69.38$, $sd = 3.70$) than females ($m = 64.50$, $sd = 2.33$), even after covarying out the effect of weight.

Practice Exercise

Using Practice Data Set 2 in Appendix B, determine if salaries are different for males and females. Repeat the analysis, statistically controlling for years of service. Write a statement of results for each. Compare and contrast your two answers.

Section 6.10   Multivariate Analysis of Variance (MANOVA)

Description

Multivariate tests are those that involve more than one **dependent variable**. While it is possible to conduct several univariate tests (one for each **dependent variable**), this causes **Type I error** inflation. Multivariate tests look at all **dependent variables** at once, in much the same way that ANOVA looks at all **levels** of an **independent variable** at once.

Assumptions

MANOVA assumes that you have multiple **dependent variables** that are related to each other. Each **dependent variable** should be normally distributed and measured on an **interval** or **ratio scale**.

SPSS Data Format

The SPSS data file should have a variable for each **dependent variable**. One additional variable is required for each between-subjects **independent variable**. It is also possible to do a MANCOVA, a repeated-measures MANOVA and a repeated-measures MANCOVA as well. These extensions require additional variables in the data file.

Running the Command

Note that this procedure requires an optional module. If you do not have this command, you do not have the proper module installed. This procedure is NOT included in the student version of SPSS.

The following data represent *SAT* and *GRE* scores for 18 participants. Six participants received no special training, six received short-term training before taking the tests, and six received long-term training. GROUP is coded 0 = no training, 1 = short-term, 2 = long-term. Enter the data and save them as SAT.sav.

SAT	GRE	GROUP
580	600	0
520	520	0
500	510	0
410	400	0
650	630	0
480	480	0
500	490	1
640	650	1
500	480	1
500	510	1
580	570	1
490	500	1
520	520	2
620	630	2
550	560	2
500	510	2
540	560	2
600	600	2

Locate the *Multivariate* command by clicking *Analyze*, then *General Linear Model*, then *Multivariate*.

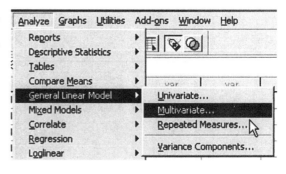

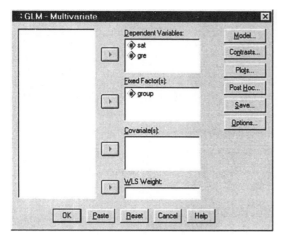

This will bring up the main **dialog box**. Enter the **dependent variables** (GRE and SAT, in this case) in the *Dependent Variables* blank. Enter the **independent variable(s)** (GROUP, in this case) in the *Fixed Factor(s)* blank. Click *OK* to run the command.

Reading the Output

We are interested in two primary sections of output. The first one gives the results of the multivariate tests. The section labeled GROUP is the one we want. This tells us whether GROUP had an effect on any of our **dependent variables**. Four different types of multivariate test results are given. The most widely used is *Wilks' Lambda*. Thus, the answer for the MANOVA is a *Lambda* of .828, with 4 and 28 degrees of freedom. That value is not significant.

Multivariate Tests[c]

Effect		Value	F	Hypothesis df	Error df	Sig.
Intercept	Pillai's Trace	.988	569.187[a]	2.000	14.000	.000
	Wilks' Lambda	.012	569.187[a]	2.000	14.000	.000
	Hotelling's Trace	81.312	569.187[a]	2.000	14.000	.000
	Roy's Largest Root	81.312	569.187[a]	2.000	14.000	.000
group	Pillai's Trace	.174	.713	4.000	30.000	.590
	Wilks' Lambda	.828	.693[a]	4.000	28.000	.603
	Hotelling's Trace	.206	.669	4.000	26.000	.619
	Roy's Largest Root	.196	1.469[b]	2.000	15.000	.261

a. Exact statistic

b. The statistic is an upper bound on F that yields a lower bound on the significance level.

c. Design: Intercept+group

The second section of output we want gives the results of the univariate tests (ANOVAs) for each **dependent variable**.

Tests of Between-Subjects Effects

Source	Dependent Variable	Type III Sum of Squares	df	Mean Square	F	Sig.
Corrected Model	sat	3077.778[a]	2	1538.889	.360	.703
	gre	5200.000[b]	2	2600.000	.587	.568
Intercept	sat	5205688.889	1	5205688.889	1219.448	.000
	gre	5248800.000	1	5248800.000	1185.723	.000
group	sat	3077.778	2	1538.889	.360	.703
	gre	5200.000	2	2600.000	.587	.568
Error	sat	64033.333	15	4268.889		
	gre	66400.000	15	4426.667		
Total	sat	5272800.000	18			
	gre	5320400.000	18			
Corrected Total	sat	67111.111	17			
	gre	71600.000	17			

a. R Squared = .046 (Adjusted R Squared = -.081)

b. R Squared = .073 (Adjusted R Squared = -.051)

Drawing Conclusions

We interpret the results of the univariate tests only if the group *Wilks' Lambda* is significant. Our results are not significant, but we will first consider how to interpret results that are significant.

Phrasing Results That Are Significant

If we had received the following output instead, we would have had a significant MANOVA, and we could state the following:

Multivariate Tests^c

Effect		Value	F	Hypothesis df	Error df	Sig.
Intercept	Pillai's Trace	.989	643.592ᵃ	2.000	14.000	.000
	Wilks' Lambda	.011	643.592ᵃ	2.000	14.000	.000
	Hotelling's Trace	91.942	643.592ᵃ	2.000	14.000	.000
	Roy's Largest Root	91.942	643.592ᵃ	2.000	14.000	.000
group	Pillai's Trace	.579	3.059	4.000	30.000	.032
	Wilks' Lambda	.423	3.757ᵃ	4.000	28.000	.014
	Hotelling's Trace	1.355	4.404	4.000	26.000	.008
	Roy's Largest Root	1.350	10.125ᵇ	2.000	15.000	.002

a. Exact statistic

b. The statistic is an upper bound on F that yields a lower bound on the significance level.

c. Design: Intercept+group

Tests of Between-Subjects Effects

Source	Dependent Variable	Type III Sum of Squares	df	Mean Square	F	Sig.
Corrected Model	sat	62077.778ᵃ	2	31038.889	7.250	.006
	gre	86344.444ᵇ	2	43172.222	9.465	.002
Intercept	sat	5859605.556	1	5859605.556	1368.711	.000
	gre	5997338.889	1	5997338.889	1314.886	.000
group	sat	62077.778	2	31038.889	7.250	.006
	gre	86344.444	2	43172.222	9.465	.002
Error	sat	64216.667	15	4281.111		
	gre	68416.667	15	4561.111		
Total	sat	5985900.000	18			
	gre	6152100.000	18			
Corrected Total	sat	126294.444	17			
	gre	154761.111	17			

A one-way MANOVA was calculated examining the effect of training (none, short-term, long-term) on *SAT* and *GRE* scores. A significant effect was found (*Lambda*(4,28) = .423, *p* = .014). Follow-up univariate ANOVAs indicated that *SAT* scores were significantly improved by training (*F*(2,15) = 7.250, *p* = .006). *GRE* scores were also significantly improved by training (*F*(2,15) = 9.465, *p* = .002).

Phrasing Results That Are Not Significant

The actual example presented was not significant. Therefore, we could state the following in the results section:

A one-way MANOVA was calculated examining the effect of training (none, short-term, or long-term) on *SAT* and *GRE* scores. No significant effect was found (*Lambda*(4,28) = .828, *p* > .05). Neither *SAT* nor *GRE* scores were significantly influenced by training.

Chapter 7

Nonparametric Inferential Statistics

Nonparametric tests are used when the corresponding parametric procedure is inappropriate. Normally, this is because the **dependent variable** is not **interval-** or **ratio-scaled**. It can also be because the **dependent variable** is not normally distributed. If the data of interest are frequency counts, nonparametric statistics may also be appropriate.

Section 7.1 Chi-Square Goodness of Fit

Description

The chi-square goodness of fit test determines whether or not sample proportions match the theoretical values. For example, it could be used to determine if a die is "loaded" or fair. It could also be used to compare the proportion of children born with birth defects to the population value (e.g., to determine if a certain neighborhood has a statistically higher-than-normal rate of birth defects).

Assumptions

We need to make very few assumptions. There are no assumptions about the shape of the distribution. The expected frequencies for each category should be at least 1, and no more than 20% of the categories should have expected frequencies of less than 5.

SPSS Data Format

SPSS requires only a single variable.

Running the Command

We will create the following data set and call it COINS.sav. The following data represent the flipping of each of two coins 20 times (H is coded as heads, T as tails).

Coin 1: H T H H T H H T H H H H T T T H T H T T H
Coin 2: T T H H T H T H T T H H H T H H H T H T H H

Name the two variables COIN1 and COIN2, and code H as 1 and T as 2. The data file that you create will have 20 rows of data and two columns, called COIN1 and COIN2.

To run the *Chi-Square* command, click *Analyze*, then *Nonparametric Tests*, then *Chi-Square*. This will bring up the main **dialog box** for the Chi-Square Test.

Transfer the variable COIN1 into the *Test Variable List*. A "fair" coin has an equal chance of coming up heads or tails. Therefore, we will leave the *Expected Values* set to *All categories equal*.

We could test a specific set of proportions by entering the relative frequencies in the *Expected Values* area. Click *OK* to run the analysis.

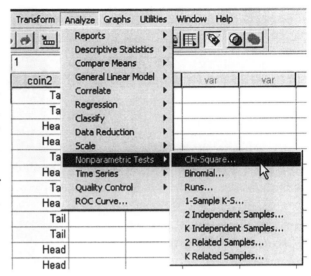

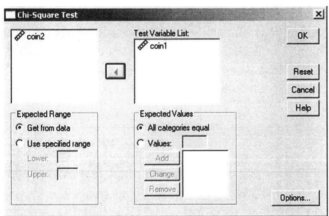

Reading the Output

The output consists of two sections. The first section gives the frequencies (observed *N*) of each value of the variable. The expected value is given, along with the difference of the observed from the expected value (called the residual). In our example, with 20 flips of a coin, we should get 10 of each value.

COIN1

	Observed N	Expected N	Residual
Head	11	10.0	1.0
Tail	9	10.0	-1.0
Total	20		

The second section of the output gives the results of the chi-square test.

Test Statistics

	coin1
Chi-Square[a]	.200
df	1
Asymp. Sig.	.655

a. 0 cells (.0%) have expected frequencies less than 5. The minimum expected cell frequency is 10.0.

Drawing Conclusions

A significant chi-square test indicates that the data vary from the expected values. A test that is not significant indicates that the data are consistent with the expected values.

Phrasing Results That Are Significant

In describing the results, you should state the value of chi-square (whose symbol is χ^2), the degrees of freedom, the **significance** level, and a description of the results. For example, with a significant chi-square (for a sample different from the example above, such as if we had used a "loaded" die), we could state the following:

> A chi-square goodness of fit test was calculated comparing the frequency of occurrence of each value of a die. It was hypothesized that each value would occur an equal number of times. Significant deviation from the hypothesized values was found ($\chi^2(5) = 25.48$, $p < .05$). The die appears to be "loaded."

Note that this example uses hypothetical values.

Phrasing Results That Are Not Significant

If the analysis produces no significant difference, as in the previous example, we could state the following:

> A chi-square goodness of fit test was calculated comparing the frequency of occurrence of heads and tails on a coin. It was hypothesized that each value would occur an equal number of times. No significant deviation from the hypothesized values was found ($\chi^2(1) = .20$, $p > .05$). The coin appears to be fair.

Practice Exercise

Use Practice Data Set 2 in Appendix B. In the entire population from which the sample was drawn, 20% of employees are clerical, 50% are technical, and 30% are professional. Determine whether or not the sample drawn conforms to these values. HINT: Enter the relative proportions of the three samples in order (20, 50, 30) in the "Expected Values" area.

Section 7.2   Chi-Square Test of Independence

Description

The chi-square test of independence tests whether or not two variables are independent of each other. For example, flips of a coin should be **independent events**, so knowing the outcome of one coin toss should not tell us anything about the second coin toss. The chi-square test of independence is essentially a nonparametric version of the **interaction** term in ANOVA.

Assumptions

Very few assumptions are needed. For example, we make no assumptions about the shape of the distribution. The expected frequencies for each category should be at least 1, and no more than 20% of the categories should have expected frequencies of less than 5.

SPSS Data Format

At least two variables are required.

Running the Command

The chi-square test of independence is a component of the *Crosstabs* command. For more details, see the section in Chapter 3 on frequency distributions for more than one variable.

This example uses the COINS.sav example. COIN1 is placed in the *Row(s)* blank, and COIN2 is placed in the *Column(s)* blank.

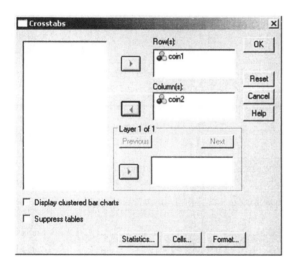

Click *Statistics*, then check the *Chi-square* box. Click *Continue*. You may also want to click *Cells* to select expected frequencies in addition to observed frequencies, as we will do on the next page. Click *OK* to run the analysis.

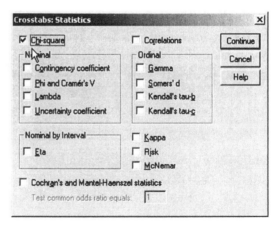

Reading the Output

The output consists of two parts. The first part gives you the counts. In this example, the actual and expected frequencies are shown because they were selected with the *Cells* option.

COIN1 * COIN2 Crosstabulation

			COIN2 Head	COIN2 Tail	Total
COIN1	Head	Count	7	4	11
		Expected Count	6.1	5.0	11.0
	Tail	Count	4	5	9
		Expected Count	5.0	4.1	9.0
Total		Count	11	9	20
		Expected Count	11.0	9.0	20.0

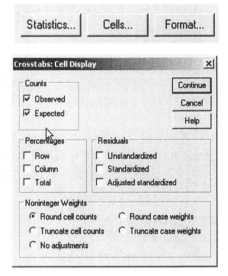

Note that you can also use the *Cells* option to display the percentages of each variable that are each value. This is especially useful when your groups are different sizes.

The second part of the output gives the results of the chi-square test. The most commonly used value is the Pearson chi-square, shown in the first row (value of .737).

Chi-Square Tests

	Value	df	Asymp. Sig. (2-sided)	Exact Sig. (2-sided)	Exact Sig. (1-sided)
Pearson Chi-Square	.737[b]	1	.391		
Continuity Correction[a]	.165	1	.684		
Likelihood Ratio	.740	1	.390		
Fisher's Exact Test				.653	.342
Linear-by-Linear Association	.700	1	.403		
N of Valid Cases	20				

[a.] Computed only for a 2x2 table

[b.] 3 cells (75.0%) have expected count less than 5. The minimum expected count is 4.05.

Drawing Conclusions

A significant chi-square test result indicates that the two variables are not independent. A value that is not significant indicates that the variables do not vary significantly from independence.

Phrasing Results That Are Significant

In describing the results, you should give the value of chi-square, the degrees of freedom, the **significance** level, and a description of the results. For example, with a significant chi-square (for a data set different from the one discussed above), we could state the following:

A chi-square test of independence was calculated comparing the frequency of heart disease in men and women. A significant interaction was found ($\chi^2(1) =$ 23.80, $p < .05$). Men were more likely to get heart disease (68%) than were women (40%).

Note that this summary statement assumes that a test was run in which participants' sex, as well as whether or not they had heart disease, was coded.

Phrasing Results That Are Not Significant

A chi-square test that is not significant indicates that there is no significant dependence of one variable on the other. The coin example above was not significant. Therefore, we could state the following:

A chi-square test of independence was calculated comparing the result of flipping two coins. No significant relationship was found ($\chi^2(1) = .737$, $p >$ .05). Flips of a coin appear to be independent events.

Practice Exercise

A researcher wants to know whether or not individuals are more likely to help in an emergency when they are indoors than when they are outdoors. Of 28 participants who were outdoors, 19 helped and 9 did not. Of 23 participants who were indoors, 8 helped and 15 did not. Enter these data, and find out if helping behavior is affected by the environment. The key to this problem is in the data entry. (Hint: How many participants were there, and what do you know about each participant?)

Section 7.3 Mann-Whitney *U* Test

Description

The Mann-Whitney *U* test is the nonparametric equivalent of the independent *t* test. It tests whether or not two independent samples are from the same distribution. The Mann-Whitney *U* test is weaker than the independent *t* test, and the *t* test should be used if you can meet its assumptions.

Assumptions

The Mann-Whitney *U* test uses the rankings of the data. Therefore, the data for the two samples must be at least **ordinal**. There are no assumptions about the shape of the distribution.

SPSS Data Format

This command requires a single variable representing the **dependent variable** and a second variable indicating group membership.

Running the Command

This example will use a new data file. It represents 12 participants in a series of races. There were long races, medium races, and short races. Participants either had a lot of experience (2), some experience (1), or no experience (0).

Enter the data from the figure at right in a new file, and save the data file as RACE.sav. The values for LONG, MEDIUM, and SHORT represent the results of the race, with 1 being first place and 12 being last.

	long	medium	short	experience
1	1	4	6	2
2	2	3	4	2
3	3	2	7	2
4	4	5	3	2
5	5	1	10	1
6	6	8	5	1
7	7	7	12	1
8	8	6	1	1
9	9	10	3	0
10	10	9	9	0
11	11	11	11	0
12	12	12	2	0

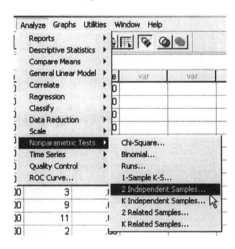

To run the command, click *Analyze*, then *Nonparametric Tests*, then *2 Independent Samples*. This will bring up the main **dialog box**.

Enter the **dependent variable** (LONG, for this example) in the *Test Variable List* blank. Enter the **independent variable** (EXPERIENCE) as the *Grouping Variable*. Make sure that *Mann-Whitney U* is checked.

Click *Define Groups* to select which two groups you will compare. For this example, we will compare those runners with no experience (0) to those runners with a lot of experience (2). Click *OK* to run the analysis.

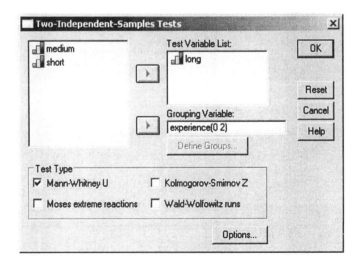

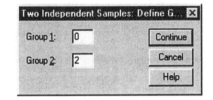

Reading the Output

The output consists of two sections. The first section gives **descriptive statistics** for the two samples. Because the data are only required to be **ordinal**, summaries relating to their ranks are used. Those participants who had no experience averaged 6.5 as their place in the race. Those participants with a lot of experience averaged 2.5 as their place in the race.

Ranks

	experience	N	Mean Rank	Sum of Ranks
long	.00	4	6.50	26.00
	2.00	4	2.50	10.00
	Total	8		

The second section of the output is the result of the Mann-Whitney U test itself. The value obtained was 0.0, with a **significance** level of .021.

Test Statistics[b]

	long
Mann-Whitney U	.000
Wilcoxon W	10.000
Z	-2.309
Asymp. Sig. (2-tailed)	.021
Exact Sig. [2*(1-tailed Sig.)]	.029[a]

a. Not corrected for ties.

b. Grouping Variable: experience

Drawing Conclusions

A significant Mann-Whitney U result indicates that the two samples are different in terms of their average ranks.

Phrasing Results That Are Significant

Our example above is significant, so we could state the following:

A Mann-Whitney U test was calculated examining the place that runners with varying levels of experience took in a long-distance race. Runners with no experience did significantly worse (*m* place = 6.50) than runners with a lot of experience (*m* place = 2.50; $U = 0.00$, $p < .05$).

Phrasing Results That Are Not Significant

If we conduct the analysis on the short-distance race instead of the long-distance race, we will get the following results, which are not significant.

Ranks

	experience	N	Mean Rank	Sum of Ranks
short	.00	4	4.63	18.50
	2.00	4	4.38	17.50
	Total	8		

Test Statistics[b]

	short
Mann-Whitney U	7.500
Wilcoxon W	17.500
Z	-.145
Asymp. Sig. (2-tailed)	.885
Exact Sig. [2*(1-tailed Sig.)]	.886[a]

a. Not corrected for ties.

b. Grouping Variable: experience

Therefore, we could state the following:

A Mann-Whitney *U* test was used to examine the difference in the race performance of runners with no experience and runners with a lot of experience in a short-distance race. No significant difference in the results of the race was found (*U* = 7.50, *p* > .05). Runners with no experience averaged a place of 4.63. Runners with a lot of experience averaged 4.38.

Practice Exercise

Assume that the mathematics scores in Practice Exercise 1 (Appendix B) are measured on an **ordinal scale**. Determine if younger participants (< 26) have significantly lower mathematics scores than older participants.

Section 7.4   Wilcoxon Test

Description

The Wilcoxon test is the nonparametric equivalent of the paired-samples (dependent) *t* test. It tests whether or not two related samples are from the same distribution. The Wilcoxon test is weaker than the independent *t* test, so the *t* test should be used if you can meet its assumptions.

Assumptions

The Wilcoxon test is based on the difference in rankings. The data for the two samples must be at least **ordinal**. There are no assumptions about the shape of the distribution.

SPSS Data Format

The test requires two variables. One variable represents the **dependent variable** at one level of the **independent variable**. The other variable represents the **dependent variable** at the second level of the **independent variable**.

Running the Command

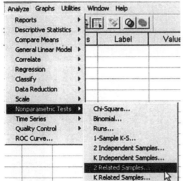

Locate the command by clicking *Analyze*, then *Nonparametric Tests*, then *2 Related Samples*. This example uses the RACE.sav data set.

This will bring up the **dialog box** for the Wilcoxon test. Note the similarity between it and the **dialog box**

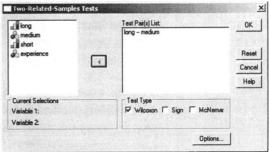

for the dependent *t* test. If you have trouble, refer to Section 6.4 on the dependent (paired-samples) *t* test in Chapter 6.

Transfer the variables LONG and MEDIUM as a pair and click *OK* to run the test. This will determine if the runners perform equivalently on long- and medium-distance races.

Reading the Output

The output consists of two parts. The first part gives summary statistics for the two variables. The second section contains the result of the Wilcoxon test (given as Z).

Ranks

		N	Mean Rank	Sum of Ranks
MEDIUM - LONG	Negative Ranks	4[a]	5.38	21.50
	Positive Ranks	5[b]	4.70	23.50
	Ties	3[c]		
	Total	12		

a. MEDIUM < LONG

b. MEDIUM > LONG

c. LONG = MEDIUM

Test Statistics[b]

	MEDIUM - LONG
Z	-.121[a]
Asymp. Sig. (2-tailed)	.904

a. Based on negative ranks.

b. Wilcoxon Signed Ranks Test

The example above shows that no significant difference was found between the results of the long-distance and medium-distance races.

Phrasing Results That Are Significant

A significant result means that a change has occurred between the two measurements. If that happened, we could state the following:

A Wilcoxon test examined the results of the medium-distance and long-distance races. A significant difference was found in the results ($Z = 3.40$, $p < .05$). Medium-distance results were better than long-distance results.

Note that these results are fictitious.

Phrasing Results That Are Not Significant

In fact, the results in the example above were not significant, so we could state the following:

A Wilcoxon test examined the results of the medium-distance and long-distance races. No significant difference was found in the results ($Z = -0.121$, $p > .05$). Medium-distance results were not significantly different from long-distance results.

Practice Exercise

Use the RACE.sav data file to determine whether or not the outcome of short-distance races is different from that of medium-distance races. Phrase your results.

Section 7.5 Kruskal-Wallis *H* Test

Description

The Kruskal-Wallis *H* test is the nonparametric equivalent of the one-way ANOVA. It tests whether or not several independent samples come from the same population.

Assumptions

Because the test is nonparametric, there are very few assumptions. However, the test does assume an **ordinal** level of measurement for the **dependent variable**. The **independent variable** should be **nominal** or **ordinal**.

SPSS Data Format

SPSS requires one variable to represent the **dependent variable** and another to represent the **levels** of the **independent variable**.

Running the Command

This example uses the RACE.sav data file. To run the command, click *Analyze*, then *Nonparametric Tests*, then *K Independent Samples*. This will bring up the main **dialog box**.

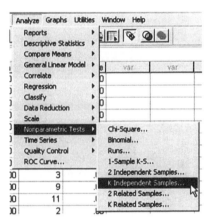

Enter the **independent variable** (EXPERIENCE) as the *Grouping Variable*, and click *Define Range* to define the lowest (0) and highest (2) values. Enter the **dependent variable** (LONG) in the *Test Variable List*, and click *OK*.

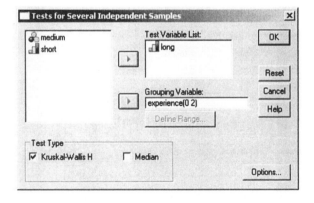

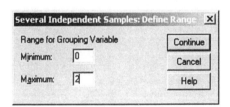

Reading the Output

The output consists of two parts. The first part gives summary statistics for each of the groups defined by the grouping (independent) variable.

Ranks

	experience	N	Mean Rank
long	.00	4	10.50
	1.00	4	6.50
	2.00	4	2.50
	Total	12	

The second part of the output gives the results of the Kruskal-Wallis test (given as a chi-square value, but we will describe it as an *H*). The example here is a significant value of 9.846.

Test Statistics^{a,b}

	long
Chi-Square	9.846
df	2
Asymp. Sig.	.007

a. Kruskal Wallis Test

b. Grouping Variable: experience

Drawing Conclusions

Like the one-way ANOVA, the Kruskal-Wallis test assumes that the groups are equal. Thus, a significant result indicates that at least one of the groups is different from at least one other group. Unlike the *One-Way ANOVA* command, however, there are no options available for post-hoc analysis.

Phrasing Results That Are Significant

The example above is significant, so we could state the following:

A Kruskal-Wallis test was conducted comparing the outcome of a long-distance race for runners with varying levels of experience. A significant result was found ($H(2) = 9.85$, $p < .01$), indicating that the groups differed from each other. Runners with no experience averaged a placement of 10.50, while runners with some experience averaged 6.50 and runners with a lot of experience averaged 2.50. The more experience the runners had, the better they performed.

Phrasing Results That Are Not Significant

If we conducted the analysis using the results of the short-distance race, we would get the following output, which is not significant.

Ranks

	experience	N	Mean Rank
short	.00	4	6.38
	1.00	4	7.25
	2.00	4	5.88
	Total	12	

Test Statistics^{a,b}

	short
Chi-Square	.299
df	2
Asymp. Sig.	.861

a. Kruskal Wallis Test

b. Grouping Variable: experience

This result is not significant, so we could state the following:

A Kruskal-Wallis test was conducted comparing the outcome of a short-distance race for runners with varying levels of experience. No significant difference was found ($H(2) = 0.299$, $p > .05$), indicating that the groups did not differ significantly from each other. Runners with no experience averaged a placement of 6.38, while runners with some experience averaged 7.25 and runners with a lot of experience averaged 5.88. Experience did not seem to influence the results of the short-distance race.

Practice Exercise

Use Practice Data Set 2 in Appendix B. Job classification is **ordinal** (clerical < technical < professional). Determine if males and females have differing **levels** of job classifications. Phrase your results.

Section 7.6   Friedman Test

Description

The Friedman test is the nonparametric equivalent of a one-way repeated-measures ANOVA. It is used when you have more than two measurements from related participants.

Assumptions

The test uses the rankings of the variables, so the data must be at least **ordinal**. No other assumptions are required.

SPSS Data Format

SPSS requires at least three variables in the SPSS data file. Each variable represents the **dependent variable** at one of the **levels** of the **independent variable**.

Running the Command

Locate the command by clicking *Analyze*, then *Nonparametric Tests*, then *K Related Samples*. This will bring up the main **dialog box**.

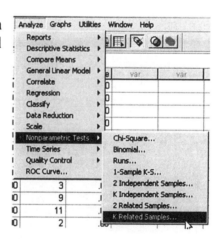

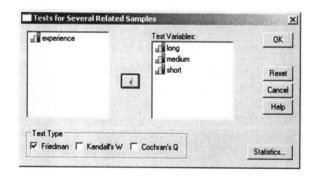

Place all the variables representing the **levels** of the **independent variable** in the *Test Variables* area. For this example, use the RACE.sav data file and the variables LONG, MEDIUM, and SHORT. Click *OK*.

Reading the Output

The output consists of two sections. The first section gives you summary statistics for each of the variables. The second section of the output gives you the results of the test as a chi-square value. The example here has a value of 0.049 and is not significant (Asymp. Sig., otherwise known as p, is .976, which is greater than .05).

Ranks

	Mean Rank
LONG	2.00
MEDIUM	2.04
SHORT	1.96

Test Statistics[a]

N	12
Chi-Square	.049
df	2
Asymp. Sig.	.976

a. Friedman Test

Drawing Conclusions

The Friedman test assumes that the three variables are from the same population. A significant value indicates that the variables are not equivalent.

Phrasing Results That Are Significant

If we obtained a significant result, we could state the following (these are hypothetical results):

A Friedman test was conducted comparing the average place in a race of runners for short-distance, medium-distance, and long-distance races. A significant difference was found ($\chi^2(2) = 0.057$, $p < .05$). The length of the race significantly affects the results of the race.

Phrasing Results That Are Not Significant

In fact, the example above was not significant, so we could state the following:

A Friedman test was conducted comparing the average place in a race of runners for short-distance, medium-distance, and long-distance races. No significant difference was found ($\chi^2(2) = 0.049$, $p > .05$). The length of the race did not significantly affect the results of the race.

Practice Exercise

Use the data in Practice Data Set 3 in Appendix B. If anxiety is measured on an **ordinal** scale, determine if anxiety levels changed over time. Phrase your results.

Chapter 8

Test Construction

Section 8.1 Item-Total Analysis

Description

Item-total analysis is a way to assess the **internal consistency** of a data set. As such, it is one of many tests of **reliability**. Item-total analysis comprises a number of items that make up a scale or test designed to measure a single construct (e.g., intelligence), and determines the degree to which all of the items measure the same construct. It does not tell you if it is measuring the correct construct (that is a question of **validity**). Before a test can be valid, however, it must first be reliable.

Assumptions

All the items in the scale should be measured on an **interval** or **ratio scale**. In addition, each item should be normally distributed. If your items are **ordinal** in nature, you can conduct the analysis using the Spearman *rho* correlation instead of the Pearson *r* correlation.

SPSS Data Format

SPSS requires one variable for each item (or question) in the scale. In addition, you must have a variable representing the total score for the scale.

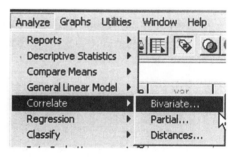

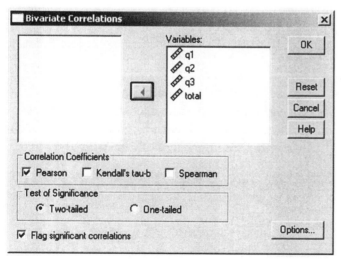

Conducting the Test

Item-total analysis uses the *Pearson Correlation* command. To conduct it, open the QUESTIONS.sav data file you created in Chapter 2. Click *Analyze*, then *Correlate*, then *Bivariate*.

Place all questions and the total in the right-hand window, and click *OK*. (For more help on conducting correlations, see Chapter 5.) The total can be calculated with the techniques discussed in Chapter 2.

Reading the Output

The output consists of a **correlation matrix** containing all questions and the total. Use the column labeled TOTAL, and locate the correlation between the total score and each question. In the example at right, Question 1 has a correlation of 0.873 with the total score. Question 2 has a correlation of −0.130 with the total. Question 3 has a correlation of 0.926 with the total.

Correlations

		Q1	Q2	Q3	TOTAL
Q1	Pearson Correlation	1.000	-.447	.718	.873
	Sig. (2-tailed)	.	.553	.282	.127
	N	4	4	4	4
Q2	Pearson Correlation	-.447	1.000	-.229	-.130
	Sig. (2-tailed)	.553	.	.771	.870
	N	4	4	4	4
Q3	Pearson Correlation	.718	-.229	1.000	.926
	Sig. (2-tailed)	.282	.771	.	.074
	N	4	4	4	4
TOTAL	Pearson Correlation	.873	-.130	.926	1.000
	Sig. (2-tailed)	.127	.870	.074	.
	N	4	4	4	4

Interpreting the Output

Item-total correlations should always be positive. If you obtain a negative correlation, that question should be removed from the scale (or you may consider whether it should be reverse-keyed).

Generally, item-total correlations of greater than 0.7 are considered desirable. Those of less than 0.3 are considered weak. Any questions with correlations of less than 0.3 should be removed from the scale.

Normally, the worst question is removed, then the total is recalculated. After the total is recalculated, the item-total analysis is repeated without the question that was removed. Then, if any questions have correlations of less than 0.3, the worst one is removed, and the process is repeated.

When all remaining correlations are greater than 0.3, the remaining items in the scale are considered to be those that are internally consistent.

Section 8.2 Cronbach's Alpha

Description

Cronbach's alpha is a measure of **internal consistency**. As such, it is one of many tests of **reliability**. Cronbach's alpha comprises a number of items that make up a scale designed to measure a single construct (e.g., intelligence), and determines the degree to which all the items are measuring the same construct. It does not tell you if it is measuring the correct construct (that is a question of **validity**). Before a test can be valid, however, it must first be reliable.

Assumptions

All the items in the scale should be measured on an **interval** or **ratio scale**. In addition, each item should be normally distributed.

SPSS Data Format

SPSS requires one variable for each item (or question) in the scale.

Running the Command

This example uses the QUEST-IONS.sav data file we first created in Chapter 2. Click *Analyze*, then *Scale*, then *Reliability Analysis*.

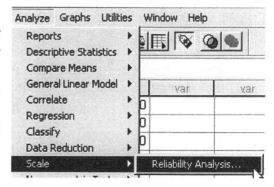

This will bring up the main **dialog box** for Reliability Analysis. Transfer the questions from your scale to the *Items* blank, and click *OK*. Do not transfer any variables representing total scores.

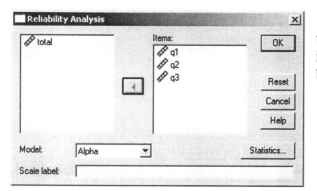

Note that when you change the options under *Model*, additional measures of **internal consistency** (e.g., split-half) can be calculated.

Reading the Output

In this example, the **reliability** coefficient is 0.407. Numbers close to 1.00 are very good, but numbers close to 0.00 represent poor **internal consistency**.

Reliability Statistics

Cronbach's Alpha	N of Items
.407	3

Section 8.3   Test–Retest Reliability

Description

Test–retest reliability is a measure of **temporal stability**. As such, it is a measure of **reliability**. Unlike measures of **internal consistency** that tell you the extent to which all of the questions that make up a scale measure the same construct, measures of **temporal stability** tell you whether or not the instrument is consistent over time and/or over multiple administrations.

Assumptions

The total score for the scale should be an **interval** or **ratio scale**. The scale scores should be normally distributed.

SPSS Data Format

SPSS requires a variable representing the total score for the scale at the time of first administration. A second variable representing the total score for the same participants at a different time (normally two weeks later) is also required.

Running the Command

The test–retest reliability coefficient is simply a Pearson correlation coefficient for the relationship between the total scores for the two administrations. To compute the coefficient, follow the directions for computing a Pearson correlation coefficient (Chapter 5, Section 5.1). Use the two variables representing the two administrations of the test.

Reading the Output

The correlation between the two scores is the test–retest reliability coefficient. It should be positive. Strong **reliability** is indicated by values close to 1.00. Weak **reliability** is indicated by values close to 0.00.

Section 8.4   Criterion-Related Validity

Description

Criterion-related validity determines the extent to which the scale you are testing correlates with a criterion. For example, *ACT* scores should correlate highly with GPA. If they do, that is a measure of **validity** for *ACT* scores. If they do not, that indicates that *ACT* scores may not be valid for the intended purpose.

Assumptions

All of the same assumptions for the Pearson correlation coefficient apply to measures of criterion-related validity (**interval** or **ratio scales**, **normal distribution**, etc.).

SPSS Data Format

Two variables are required. One variable represents the total score for the scale you are testing. The other represents the criterion you are testing it against.

Running the Command

Calculating criterion-related validity involves determining the Pearson correlation value between the scale and the criterion. See Chapter 5, Section 5.1 for complete information.

Reading the Output

The correlation between the two scores is the criterion-related validity coefficient. It should be positive. Strong **validity** is indicated by values close to 1.00. Weak **validity** is indicated by values close to 0.00.

Appendix A

Effect Size

Many disciplines are placing increased emphasis on reporting **effect size**. While statistical hypothesis testing provides a way to tell the odds that differences are real, effect sizes provide a way to judge the relative importance of those differences. That is, they tell us the size of the difference or relationship. They are also critical if you would like to estimate necessary sample sizes, conduct a power analysis, or conduct a meta-analysis. Many professional organizations (e.g., the American Psychological Association) are now requiring or strongly suggesting that effect sizes be reported in addition to the results of hypothesis tests.

Because there are at least 41 different types of effect sizes,[1] each with somewhat different properties, the purpose of this Appendix is not to be a comprehensive resource on **effect size**, but rather to show you how to calculate some of the most common measures of **effect size** using SPSS 15.0.

Cohen's *d*

One of the simplest and most popular measures of **effect size** is **Cohen's *d***. **Cohen's *d*** is a member of a class of measurements called "standardized mean differences." In essence, *d* is the difference between the two means divided by the overall **standard deviation**.

It is not only a popular measure of **effect size**, but Cohen has also suggested a simple basis to interpret the value obtained. Cohen[2] suggested that effect sizes of .2 are small, .5 are medium, and .8 are large.

We will discuss **Cohen's *d*** as the preferred measure of **effect size** for *t* tests. Unfortunately, SPSS does not calculate **Cohen's *d***. However, this appendix will cover how to calculate it from the output that SPSS does produce.

Effect Size for Single-Sample t Tests

Although SPSS does not calculate **effect size** for the single-sample *t* test, calculating **Cohen's *d*** is a simple matter.

---

[1] Kirk, R.E. (1996). Practical significance: A concept whose time has come. *Educational & Psychological Measurement, 56,* 746–759.
[2] Cohen, J. (1992). A power primer. *Psychological Bulletin, 112,* 155–159.

T-Test

One-Sample Statistics

	N	Mean	Std. Deviation	Std. Error Mean
LENGTH	10	35 9000	1.1972	3786

One-Sample Test

	Test Value = 35					
					95% Confidence Interval of the Difference	
	t	df	Sig (2-tailed)	Mean Difference	Lower	Upper
LENGTH	2 377	9	041	9000	4 356E-02	1 7564

Cohen's *d* for a single-sample *t* test is equal to the **mean** difference over the **standard deviation**. If SPSS provides us with the following output, we calculate *d* as indicated here:

$$d = \frac{\overline{D}}{s_D}$$

$$d = \frac{.90}{1.1972}$$

$$d = .752$$

In this example, using Cohen's guidelines to judge **effect size**, we would have an **effect size** between medium and large.

Effect Size for Independent-Samples t Tests

Calculating **effect size** from the independent *t* test output is a little more complex because SPSS does not provide us with the **pooled standard deviation**. The upper section of the output, however, does provide us with the information we need to calculate it. The output presented here is the same output we worked with in Chapter 6.

Group Statistics

	morning	N	Mean	Std. Deviation	Std. Error Mean
grade	No	2	82.5000	3.53553	2.50000
	Yes	2	78.0000	7.07107	5.00000

$$s_{pooled} = \sqrt{\frac{(n_1 - 1)s_1^2 + (n_2 - 1)s_2^2}{n_1 + n_2 - 2}}$$

$$s_{pooled} = \sqrt{\frac{(2-1)3.5355^2 + (2-1)7.0711^2}{2 + 2 - 2}}$$

$$s_{pooled} = \sqrt{\frac{62.500}{2}}$$

$$s_{pooled} = 5.59$$

Once we have calculated the **pooled standard deviation** (s_{pooled}), we can calculate **Cohen's *d***.

$$d = \frac{\overline{X}_1 - \overline{X}_2}{s_{pooled}}$$

$$d = \frac{82.50 - 78.00}{5.59}$$

$$d = .80$$

So, in this example, using Cohen's guidelines for the interpretation of *d*, we would have obtained a large effect size.

Effect Size for Paired-Samples t Tests

As you have probably learned in your statistics class, a paired-samples *t* test is really just a special case of the single-sample *t* test. Therefore, the procedure for calculating **Cohen's *d*** is also the same. The SPSS output, however, looks a little different, so you will be taking your values from different areas.

Paired Samples Test

		Paired Differences							
		Mean	Std. Deviation	Std. Error Mean	95% Confidence Interval of the Difference		t	df	Sig. (2-tailed)
					Lower	Upper			
Pair 1	PRETEST - FINAL	-22.8095	8.9756	1.9586	-26.8952	-18.7239	-11.646	20	.000

$$d = \frac{\overline{D}}{s_D}$$

$$d = \frac{-22.8095}{8.9756}$$

$$d = 2.54$$

Notice that in this example, we represent the **effect size** (*d*) as a positive number even though it is negative. Effect sizes are always positive numbers. In this example, using Cohen's guidelines for the interpretation of *d*, we have found a very large **effect size**.

r^2 (Coefficient of Determination)

While **Cohen's *d*** is the appropriate measure of **effect size** for *t* tests, correlation and regression effect sizes should be determined by squaring the correlation coefficient. This squared correlation is called the **coefficient of determination**. Cohen[3] suggested here that correlations of .5, .3, and .1 corresponded to large, moderate, and small relationships. Those values squared yield **coefficients of determination** of .25, .09, and .01 respectively. It would appear, therefore, that Cohen is suggesting that accounting for 25% of the variability represents a large effect, 9% a moderate effect, and 1% a small effect.

Effect Size for Correlation

Nowhere is the effect of sample size on statistical power (and therefore **significance**) more apparent than with correlations. Given a large enough sample, *any* correlation can become significant. Thus, **effect size** becomes critically important in the interpretation of correlations.

---

[3] Cohen, J. (1988). *Statistical power analysis for the behavioral sciences* (2nd ed). New Jersey: Lawrence Erlbaum.

The standard measure of **effect size** for correlations is the **coefficient of determination** (r^2) discussed above. The coefficient should be interpreted as the proportion of **variance** in the **dependent variable** that can be accounted for by the relationship between the **independent** and **dependent variables**. While Cohen provided some useful guidelines for interpretation, each problem should be interpreted in terms of its true practical **significance**. For example, if a treatment is very expensive to implement, or has significant side effects, then a larger correlation should be required before the relationship becomes "important." For treatments that are very inexpensive, a much smaller correlation can be considered "important."

To calculate the **coefficient of determination**, simply take the r value that SPSS provides and square it.

Effect Size for Regression

The Model Summary section of the output reports R^2 for you. The example output here shows a **coefficient of determination** of .649, meaning that almost 65% (.649) of the variability in the **dependent variable** is accounted for by the relationship between the **dependent** and **independent variables**.

Model Summary

Model	R	R Square	Adjusted R Square	Std. Error of the Estimate
1	.806[a]	.649	.624	16.1480

a. Predictors: (Constant), HEIGHT

Eta Squared (η^2)

A third measure of **effect size** is **Eta Squared (η^2)**. **Eta Squared** is used for Analysis of Variance models. The GLM (General Linear Model) function in SPSS (the function that runs the procedures under *Analyze—General Linear Model*) will provide **Eta Squared (η^2)**.

Eta Squared has an interpretation similar to a squared correlation coefficient (r^2). It represents the proportion of the **variance** accounted for by the effect. Unlike r^2, however, which represents only linear relationships, η^2 can represent any type of relationship.

$$\eta^2 = \frac{SS_{effect}}{SS_{effect} + SS_{error}}$$

Effect Size for Analysis of Variance

For most Analysis of Variance problems, you should elect to report **Eta Squared** as your **effect size** measure. SPSS provides this calculation for you as part of the *General Linear Model (GLM)* command.

To obtain **Eta Squared**, you simply click on the *Options* box in the main **dialog box** for the *GLM* command you are running (this works for Univariate, Multivariate, and Repeated Measures versions of the command even though only the Univariate option is presented here).

Once you have selected *Options*, a new **dialog box** will appear. One of the options in that box will be *Estimates of effect size*. When you select that box, SPSS will provide **Eta Squared** values as part of your output.

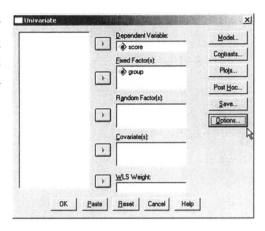

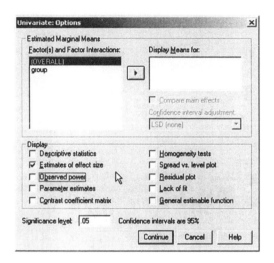

Tests of Between-Subjects Effects

Dependent Variable: score

Source	Type III Sum of Squares	df	Mean Square	F	Sig.	Partial Eta Squared
Corrected Model	10.450[a]	2	5.225	19.096	.000	.761
Intercept	91.622	1	91.622	334.862	.000	.965
group	10.450	2	5.225	19.096	.000	.761
Error	3.283	12	.274			
Total	105.000	15				
Corrected Total	13.733	14				

a. R Squared = .761 (Adjusted R Squared = .721)

In the example here, we obtained an **Eta Squared** of .761 for our main effect for group membership. Because we interpret **Eta Squared** using the same guidelines as r^2, we would conclude that this represents a large **effect size** for group membership.

Notes

Appendix B

Practice Exercise Data Sets

The practice exercises given throughout the text use a variety of data. Some practice exercises use the data sets shown in the examples. Others use longer data sets. The longer data sets are presented here.

Practice Data Set 1

You have conducted a study in which you collected data from 23 participants. You asked each subject to indicate his/her sex (SEX), age (AGE), and marital status (MARITAL). You gave each subject a test to measure mathematics skills (SKILL), where the higher scores indicate a higher skill level. The data are presented below. Note that you will have to code the variables SEX and MARITAL and also indicate that they are measured on a **nominal scale**.

SEX	AGE	MARITAL	SKILL
M	23	Single	34
F	35	Married	40
F	40	Divorced	38
M	19	Single	20
M	28	Married	30
F	35	Divorced	40
F	20	Single	38
F	29	Single	47
M	29	Married	26
M	40	Married	24
F	24	Single	45
M	23	Single	37
F	18	Single	44
M	21	Single	38
M	50	Divorced	32
F	25	Single	29
F	20	Single	38
M	24	Single	19
F	37	Married	29
M	42	Married	42
M	35	Married	59
M	23	Single	45
F	40	Divorced	20

	Name	Type	Width	Decimals	Label	Values	Missing	Columns	Align	Measure
1	sex	Numeric	8	2		{1.00, Male}...	None	8	Right	Nominal
2	age	Numeric	8	2		None	None	8	Right	Scale
3	marital	Numeric	8	2		{1.00, Single}..	None	8	Right	Nominal
4	skill	Numeric	8	2		None	None	8	Right	Scale

Practice Data Set 2

A survey of employees is conducted. Each employee provides the following information: Salary (SALARY), Years of Service (YOS), Sex (SEX), Job Classification (CLASSIFY), and Education Level (EDUC). Note that you will have to code SEX (Male = 1, Female = 2) and CLASSIFY (Clerical = 1, Technical = 2, Professional = 3).

	Name	Type	Width	Decimals	Label	Values	Missing	Columns	Align	Measure
1	salary	Numeric	8	2		None	None	8	Right	Scale
2	yos	Numeric	8	2		None	None	8	Right	Scale
3	sex	Numeric	8	2		{1.00, Male}...	None	8	Right	Nominal
4	classify	Numeric	8	2		{1.00, Clerical}	None	8	Right	Nominal
5	educ	Numeric	8	2		None	None	8	Right	Scale

SALARY	YOS	SEX	CLASSIFY	EDUC
35,000	8	Male	Technical	14
18,000	4	Female	Clerical	10
20,000	1	Male	Professional	16
50,000	20	Female	Professional	16
38,000	6	Male	Professional	20
20,000	6	Female	Clerical	12
75,000	17	Male	Professional	20
40,000	4	Female	Technical	12
30,000	8	Male	Technical	14
22,000	15	Female	Clerical	12
23,000	16	Male	Clerical	12
45,000	2	Female	Professional	16

Practice Data Set 3

Participants who have phobias are given one of three treatments (CONDITION). Their anxiety level (1 to 10) is measured at three intervals—before treatment (ANXPRE), one hour after treatment (ANX1HR), and again four hours after treatment (ANX4HR). Note that you will have to code the variable CONDITION.

	Name	Type	Width	Decimals	Label	Values	Missing	Columns	Align	Measure
1	anxpre	Numeric	8	2		None	None	8	Right	Scale
2	anx1hr	Numeric	8	2		None	None	8	Right	Scale
3	anx4hr	Numeric	8	2		None	None	8	Right	Scale
4	condit	Numeric	8	2		{1.00, Placebo	None	8	Right	Nominal

ANXPRE	ANX1HR	ANX4HR	CONDITION
8	7	7	Placebo
10	10	10	Placebo
9	7	8	Placebo
7	6	6	Placebo
7	7	7	Placebo
9	4	5	Valium™
10	6	8	Valium™
9	5	5	Valium™
8	3	5	Valium™
6	3	4	Valium™
8	5	3	Experimental Drug
6	5	2	Experimental Drug
9	8	4	Experimental Drug
10	9	4	Experimental Drug
7	6	3	Experimental Drug

7.228 11   .000 34654.6660 2401.4808

452.9026

Notes

Appendix C

Glossary

All Inclusive. A set of events that encompasses every possible outcome.

Alternative Hypothesis. The opposite of the null hypothesis, normally showing that there is a true difference. Generally, this is the statement that the researcher would like to support.

Case Processing Summary. A section of SPSS output that lists the number of subjects used in the analysis.

Coefficient of Determination. The value of the correlation, squared. It provides the proportion of variance accounted for by the relationship.

Cohen's *d*. A common and simple measure of effect size that standardizes the difference between groups.

Correlation Matrix. A section of SPSS output in which correlation coefficients are reported for all pairs of variables.

Covariate. A variable known to be related to the dependent variable, but not treated as an independent variable. Used in ANCOVA as a statistical control technique.

Data Window. The SPSS window that contains the data in a spreadsheet format. This is the window used for running most commands.

Dependent Variable. An outcome or response variable. The dependent variable is normally dependent on the independent variable.

Descriptive Statistics. Statistical procedures that organize and summarize data.

Dialog Box. A window that allows you to enter information that SPSS will use in a command.

Dichotomous Variables. Variables with only two levels (e.g., gender).

Discrete Variable. A variable that can have only certain values (i.e., values between which there is no score, like A, B, C, D, F).

Effect Size. A measure that allows one to judge the relative importance of a difference or relationship by reporting the size of a difference.

Eta Squared (η^2). A measure of effect size used in Analysis of Variance models.

Grouping Variable. In SPSS, the variable used to represent group membership. SPSS often refers to independent variables as grouping variables; SPSS sometimes refers to grouping variables as independent variables.

Independent Events. Two events are independent if information about one event gives no information about the second event (e.g., two flips of a coin).

Independent Variable. The variable whose levels (values) determine the group to which a subject belongs. A true independent variable is manipulated by the researcher. See Grouping Variable.

Inferential Statistics. Statistical procedures designed to allow the researcher to draw inferences about a population on the basis of a sample.

Interaction. With more than one independent variable, an interaction occurs when a level of one independent variable affects the influence of another independent variable.

Internal Consistency. A reliability measure that assesses the extent to which all of the items in an instrument measure the same construct.

Interval Scale. A measurement scale where items are placed in mutually exclusive categories, with equal intervals between values. Appropriate transformations include counting, sorting, and addition/subtraction.

Levels. The values that a variable can have. A variable with three levels has three possible values.

Mean. A measure of central tendency where the sum of the deviation scores equals zero.

Median. A measure of central tendency representing the middle of a distribution when the data are sorted from low to high. Fifty percent of the cases are below the median.

Mode. A measure of central tendency representing the value (or values) with the most subjects (the score with the greatest frequency).

Mutually Exclusive. Two events are mutually exclusive when they cannot occur simultaneously.

Nominal Scale. A measurement scale where items are placed in mutually exclusive categories. Differentiation is by name only (e.g., race, sex). Appropriate categories include "same" or "different." Appropriate transformations include counting.

Normal Distribution. A symmetric, unimodal, bell-shaped curve.

Null Hypothesis. The hypothesis to be tested, normally in which there is no true difference. It is mutually exclusive of the alternative hypothesis.

Ordinal Scale. A measurement scale where items are placed in mutually exclusive categories, in order. Appropriate categories include "same," "less," and "more." Appropriate transformations include counting and sorting.

Outliers. Extreme scores in a distribution. Scores that are very distant from the mean and the rest of the scores in the distribution.

Output Window. The SPSS window that contains the results of an analysis. The left side summarizes the results in an outline. The right side contains the actual results.

Percentiles (Percentile Ranks). A relative score that gives the percentage of subjects who scored at the same value or lower.

Pooled Standard Deviation. A single value that represents the standard deviation of two groups of scores.

Protected Dependent *t* Tests. To prevent the inflation of a Type I error, the level needed to be significant is reduced when multiple tests are conducted.

Quartiles. The points that define a distribution into four equal parts. The scores at the 25th, 50th, and 75th percentile ranks.

Random Assignment. A procedure for assigning subjects to conditions in which each subject has an equal chance of being assigned to any condition.

Range. A measure of dispersion representing the number of points from the highest score through the lowest score.

Ratio Scale. A measurement scale where items are placed in mutually exclusive categories, with equal intervals between values, and a true zero. Appropriate transformations include counting, sorting, addition/subtraction, and multiplication/division.

Reliability. An indication of the consistency of a scale. A reliable scale is internally consistent and stable over time.

Robust. A test is said to be robust if it continues to provide accurate results even after the violation of some assumptions.

Significance. A difference is said to be significant if the probability of making a Type I error is less than the accepted limit (normally 5%). If a difference is significant, the null hypothesis is rejected.

Skew. The extent to which a distribution is not symmetrical. Positive skew has outliers on the positive (right) side of the distribution. Negative skew has outliers on the negative (left) side of the distribution.

Standard Deviation. A measure of dispersion representing a special type of average deviation from the mean.

Standard Error of Estimate. The equivalent of the standard deviation for a regression line. The data points will be normally distributed around the regression line with a standard deviation equal to the standard error of the estimate.

Standard Normal Distribution. A normal distribution with a mean of 0.0 and a standard deviation of 1.0.

String Variable. A string variable can contain letters and numbers. Numeric variables can contain only numbers. Most SPSS commands will not function with string variables.

Temporal Stability. This is achieved when reliability measures have determined that scores remain stable over multiple administrations of the instrument.

Tukey's *HSD*. A post-hoc comparison purported to reveal an "honestly significant difference" (*HSD*).

Type I Error. A Type I error occurs when the researcher erroneously rejects the null hypothesis.

Type II Error. A Type II error occurs when the researcher erroneously fails to reject the null hypothesis.

Valid Data. Data that SPSS will use in its analyses.

Validity. An indication of the accuracy of a scale.

Variance. A measure of dispersion equal to the squared standard deviation.

Appendix D

Sample Data Files Used in Text

A variety of small data files are used in examples throughout this text. Here is a list of where each appears.

COINS.sav

Variables:	COIN1
	COIN2

Entered in Chapter 7

GRADES.sav

Variables:	PRETEST
	MIDTERM
	FINAL
	INSTRUCT
	REQUIRED

Entered in Chapter 6

HEIGHT.sav

Variables:	HEIGHT
	WEIGHT
	SEX

Entered in Chapter 4

QUESTIONS.sav

Variables:	Q1
	Q2 (recoded in Chapter 2)
	Q3
	TOTAL (added in Chapter 2)
	GROUP (added in Chapter 2)

Entered in Chapter 2
Modified in Chapter 2

RACE.sav

Variables: SHORT
MEDIUM
LONG
EXPERIENCE

Entered in Chapter 7

SAMPLE.sav

Variables: ID
DAY
TIME
MORNING
GRADE
WORK
TRAINING (added in Chapter 1)

Entered in Chapter 1
Modified in Chapter 1

SAT.sav

Variables: SAT
GRE
GROUP

Entered in Chapter 6

Other Files

For some practice exercises, see Appendix B for needed data sets that are not used in any other examples in the text.

Appendix E

Information for Users
of Earlier Versions of SPSS

There are a number of differences between SPSS 15.0 and earlier versions of the software. Fortunately, most of them have very little impact on users of this text. In fact, most users of earlier versions will be able to successfully use this text without needing to reference this appendix.

Variable names were limited to eight characters.

Versions of SPSS older than 12.0 are limited to eight-character variable names. The other variable name rules still apply. If you are using an older version of SPSS, you need to make sure you use eight or fewer letters for your variable names.

The *Data* menu will look different.

The screenshots in the text where the *Data* menu is shown will look slightly different if you are using an older version of SPSS. These missing or renamed commands do not have any effect on this text, but the menus may look slightly different.

If you are using a version of SPSS earlier than 10.0, the *Analyze* menu will be called *Statistics* instead.

Graphing functions.

Prior to SPSS 12.0, the graphing functions of SPSS were very limited. If you are using a version of SPSS older than version 12.0, third-party software like Excel or SigmaPlot is recommended for the construction of graphs. If you are using Version 14.0 of the software, use Appendix F as an alternative to Chapter 4, which discusses graphing.

Variable icons indicate measurement type.

In versions of SPSS earlier than 14.0, variables were represented in **dialog boxes** with their variable label and an icon that represented whether the variable was **string** or numeric (the example here shows all variables that were numeric).

Starting with Version 14.0, SPSS shows additional information about each variable. Icons now represent not only whether a variable is numeric or not, but also what type of measurement scale it is. **Nominal** variables are represented by the icon. **Ordinal** variables are represented by the icon. **Interval** and **ratio** variables (SPSS refers to them as scale variables) are represented by the icon.

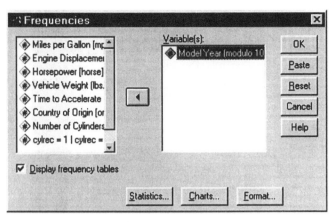

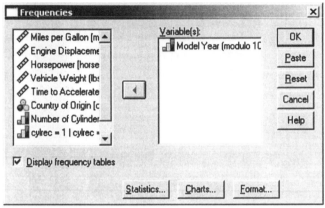

Several SPSS data files can now be open at once.

Versions of SPSS older than 14.0 could have only one data file open at a time. Copying data from one file to another entailed a tedious process of copying/opening files/pasting/etc. Starting with version 14.0, multiple data files can be open at the same time. When multiple files are open, you can select the one you want to work with using the *Window* command.

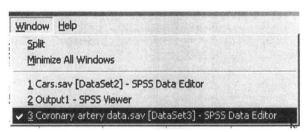

Appendix F

Graphing Data with SPSS 13.0 and 14.0

This appendix should be used as an alternative to Chapter 4 when you are using SPSS 13.0 or 14.0. These procedures may also be used in SPSS 15.0, if desired, by selecting *Legacy Dialogs* instead of *Chart Builder*.

Graphing Basics

In addition to the frequency distributions, the measures of central tendency and measures of dispersion discussed in Chapter 3, graphing is a useful way to summarize, organize, and reduce your data. It has been said that a picture is worth a thousand words. In the case of complicated data sets, that is certainly true.

With SPSS Version 13.0 and later, it is now possible to make publication-quality graphs using only SPSS. One important advantage of using SPSS instead of other software to create your graphs (e.g., Excel or SigmaPlot) is that the data have already been entered. Thus, duplication is eliminated, and the chance of making a transcription error is reduced.

Editing SPSS Graphs

Whatever command you use to create your graph, you will probably want to do some editing to make it look exactly the way you want. In SPSS, you do this in much the same way that you edit graphs in other software programs (e.g., Excel). In the **output window**, select your graph (thus creating handles around the outside of the entire object) and right-click. Then, click *SPSS Chart Object*, then click *Open*. Alternatively, you can double-click on the graph to open it for editing.

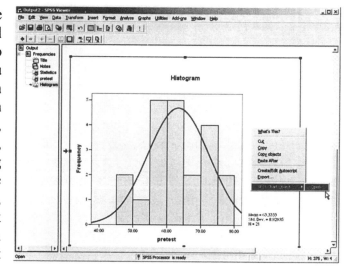

When you open the graph for editing, the *Chart Editor* window and the corresponding *Properties* window will appear.

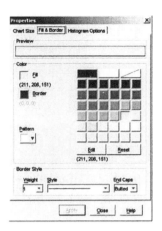

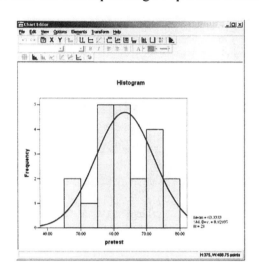

Once Chart Editor is open, you can easily edit each element of the graph. To select an element, just click on the relevant spot on the graph. For example, to select the element representing the title of the graph, click somewhere on the title (the word "Histogram" in the example below).

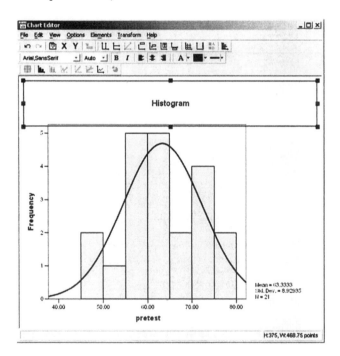

Once you have selected an element, you can tell that the correct element is selected because it will have handles around it.

If the item you have selected is a text element (e.g., the title of the graph), a cursor will be present and you can edit the text as you would in word processing programs. If you would like to change another attribute of the element (e.g., the color or font size), use the Properties box (Text properties are shown above).

With a little practice, you can make excellent graphs using SPSS. Once your graph is formatted the way you want it, simply select *File*, then *Close.*

Data Set

For the graphing examples, we will use a new set of data. Enter the data below and save the file as HEIGHT.sav. The data represent participants' HEIGHT (in inches), WEIGHT (in pounds), and SEX (1 = male, 2 = female).

HEIGHT	WEIGHT	SEX
66	150	1
69	155	1
73	160	1
72	160	1
68	150	1
63	140	1
74	165	1
70	150	1
66	110	2
64	100	2
60	95	2
67	110	2
64	105	2
63	100	2
67	110	2
65	105	2

Check that you have entered the data correctly by calculating a **mean** for each of the three variables (click *Analyze*, then *Descriptive Statistics*, then *Descriptives*). Compare your results with those in the table below.

Descriptive Statistics

	N	Minimum	Maximum	Mean	Std. Deviation
HEIGHT	16	60.00	74.00	66.9375	3.9067
WEIGHT	16	95.00	165.00	129.0625	26.3451
SEX	16	1.00	2.00	1.5000	.5164
Valid N (listwise)	16				

Bar Charts, Pie Charts, and Histograms

Description

Bar charts, pie charts, and histograms represent the number of times each score occurs by varying the height of a bar or the size of a pie piece. They are graphical representations of the frequency distributions discussed in Chapter 3.

Drawing Conclusions

The *Frequencies* command produces output that indicates both the number of cases in the sample with a particular value and the percentage of cases with that value. Thus, conclusions drawn should relate only to describing the numbers or percentages for the sample. If the data are at least **ordinal** in nature, conclusions regarding the cumulative percentages and/or **percentiles** can also be drawn.

SPSS Data Format

You need only one variable to use this command.

Running the Command

The *Frequencies* command will produce graphical frequency distributions. Click *Analyze*, then *Descriptive Statistics,* then *Frequencies.* You will be presented with the main **dialog box** for the *Frequencies* command, where you can enter the variables for which you would like to create graphs or charts. (See Chapter 3 for other options available with this command.)

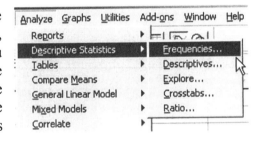

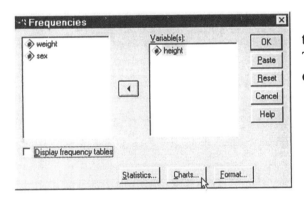

Click the *Charts* button at the bottom to produce frequency distributions. This will give you the Frequencies: Charts **dialog box**.

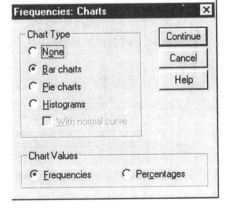

There are three types of charts under this command: *Bar charts*, *Pie charts*, and *Histograms*. For each type, the *Y* axis can be either a frequency count or a percentage (selected through the *Chart Values* option).

You will receive the charts for any variables selected in the main Frequencies command **dialog box**.

Output

The bar chart consists of a *Y* axis, representing the frequency, and an *X* axis, representing each score. Note that the only values represented on the *X* axis are those with nonzero frequencies (61, 62, and 71 are not represented).

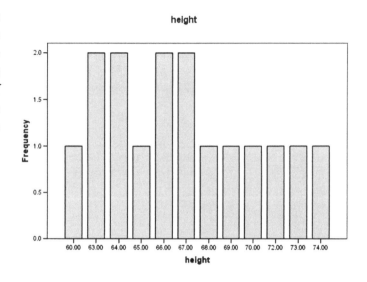

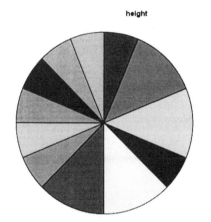

The pie chart shows the percentage of the whole that is represented by each value.

The *Histogram* command creates a grouped frequency distribution. The **range** of scores is split into evenly spaced groups. The midpoint of each group is plotted on the *X* axis, and the *Y* axis represents the number of scores for each group.

If you select *With Normal Curve*, a normal curve will be superimposed over the distribution. This is very useful for helping you determine if the distribution you have is approximately normal.

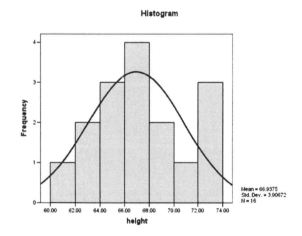

Practice Exercise

Use Practice Data Set 1 in Appendix B. After you have entered the data, construct a histogram that represents the mathematics skills scores and displays a normal curve, and a bar chart that represents the frequencies for the variable AGE.

Scatterplots

Description

Scatterplots (also called scattergrams or scatter diagrams) display two values for each case with a mark on the graph. The *X* axis represents the value for one variable. The *Y* axis represents the value for the second variable.

Assumptions

Both variables should be **interval** or **ratio scales**. If **nominal** or **ordinal** data are used, be cautious about your interpretation of the scattergram.

SPSS Data Format

You need two variables to perform this command.

Running the Command

You can produce scatterplots by clicking *Graphs*, then *Scatter/Dot*. This will give you the first Scatterplot **dialog box**. Select the desired scatterplot (normally, you will select *Simple Scatter*), then click *Define*.

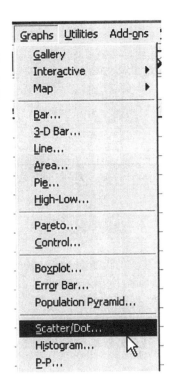

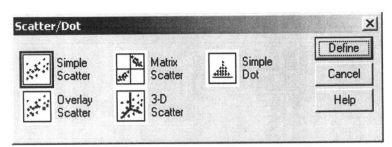

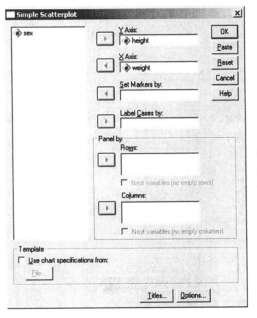

This will give you the main Scatterplot **dialog box**. Enter one of your variables as the *Y* axis and the second as the *X* axis. For example, using the HEIGHT.sav data set, enter HEIGHT as the *Y* axis and WEIGHT as the *X* axis. Click *OK*.

Output

The output will consist of a mark for each subject at the appropriate *X* and *Y* **levels**.

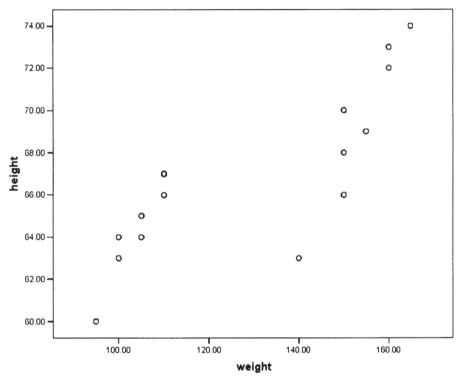

Adding a Third Variable

Even though the scatterplot is a two-dimensional graph, it can plot a third variable. To make it do so, enter the third variable in the *Set Markers by* field. In our example, we will enter the variable SEX in the *Set Markers by* space.

Now our output will have two different sets of marks. One set represents the male participants, and the second set represents the female participants. These two sets will appear in different colors on your screen. You can use the SPSS chart editor to make them different shapes, as in the graph that follows.

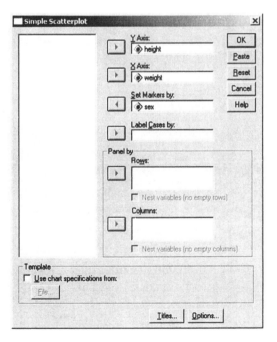

Graph

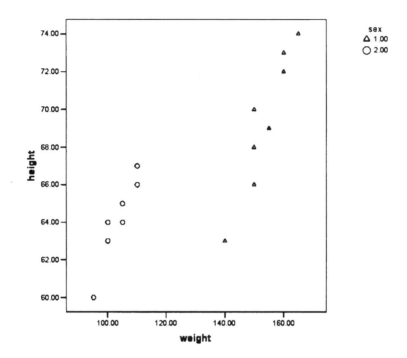

Practice Exercise

Use Practice Data Set 2 in Appendix B. Construct a scatterplot to examine the relationship between SALARY and EDUCATION.

Advanced Bar Charts

Description

You can produce bar charts with the *Frequencies* command (see Chapter 4, Section 4.3). Sometimes, however, we are interested in a bar chart where the *Y* axis is not a frequency. To produce such a chart, we need to use the *Bar Charts* command.

SPSS Data Format

At least two variables are needed to perform this command. There are two basic kinds of bar charts—those for between-subjects designs and those for repeated-measures designs. Use the between-subjects method if one variable is the **independent variable** and the other is the **dependent variable**. Use the repeated-measures method if you have a **dependent variable** for each value of the **independent variable** (e.g., you would have three variables for a design with three values of the **independent variable**). This normally occurs when you take multiple observations over time.

Running the Command

Click *Graphs*, then *Bar* for either type of bar chart. This will open the Bar Charts **dialog box**. If you have one **independent variable**, select *Simple*. If you have more than one, select *Clustered*.

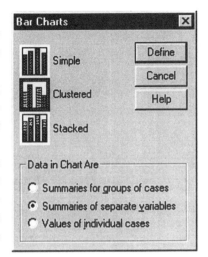

If you are using a between-subjects design, select *Summaries for groups of cases*. If you are using a repeated-measures design, select *Summaries of separate variables*.

If you are creating a repeated measures graph, you will see the **dialog box** below. Move each variable over to the *Bars Represent* area, and SPSS will place it inside parentheses following *Mean*. This will give you a graph like the one below at right. Note that this example uses the GRADES.sav data entered in Section 6.4 (Chapter 6).

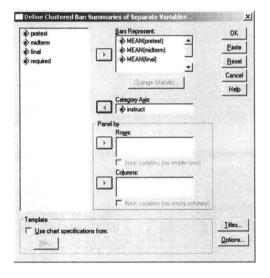

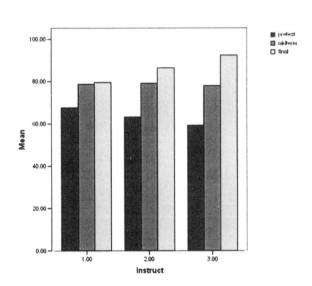

Practice Exercise

Use Practice Data Set 1 in Appendix B. Construct a bar graph examining the relationship between mathematics skills scores and marital status. Hint: In the *Bars Represent* area, enter SKILL as the variable.

Notes

Notes

Notes

Notes

Notes

Notes

Notes

- programs
- SPSS, Inc.
- PASW Statistics 18
- PASW Statistics 18
- PASW Statistics Data Editor

PASW Statistics Processor is unavailable